THE REAL TASTE OF JAMAICA

ENID DONALDSON

Photographs by Ray Chen

Warwick Publishing
Toronto Los Angeles

Contents

ACKNOWLEDGEMENTS

The publishers would like to thank the following for the loan of equipment and accessories for the photographs:

Magic Kitchen Ltd., The Village, 24 Constant Spring Road, Kingston 10 for hibiscus wooden plate p. 68, and breadfruit leaf plates p. 13

The Clonmel Potters Gallery, Shop 8, Village Plaza Kingston 10 for bowls and plate p. 36

Patoo Gallery, Upper Manor Park Plaza, Kingston 8 for wooden dishes p. 48, painted wooden chicken and eggs p. 76,plates p. 77, 122

Gifted Hands, 12 Worthington Terrace, Kingston 5 for plates p. 56

The Art Gallery, 10 Garelli Avenue, Kingston 10 for iron pot p. 59, dessert dishes p. 132

Karmen's Corner, 65⅞ Half Way Tree Road, Kingston 10, plate p. 81, dessert dishes p. 129

Gallery M.E.K., Devon House, Kingston 10 for salt and pepper shakers p. 51

Answers Gift and Home Centre, Shop 1, Tropical Plaza, Kingston 10

Things Jamaican Ltd., Bumper Hall, 68 Spanish Town Road, Kingston 14 for pottery p. 101, pewter spoon p. 31

The Antiquarian & Trading Co., Hope Road, Kingston 10.

All embroidered napkins from Allsides Workroom, 26 Parkington Plaza, Kingston 10.

Rum barrel courtesy of Dr. Ian Sangster & Co. Ltd., 17 Holborn Road, Kingston 10.

ISBN: 1-895629-64-0

Published in June 1996 by:
Warwick Publishing Inc.,
24 Mercer Street, Suite 200,
Toronto, Ontario M5V 1H3
1424 N. Highland Avenue,
Los Angeles, CA 90027

Distributed in North America by:
Firefly Books Ltd.,
3680 Victoria Park Avenue,
Willowdale, Ontario M2H 3K1

Photographs by Ray Chen

First published in 1993 by:
Ian Randle Publishers Limited
206 Old Hope Road
Kingston 6, Jamaica, W.I.

Food Stylist Donna Noble
Illustrators Natalie Butler
Juliet Thorburn
Sonia Richards
Book Design Michael Gordon
Cover Design Diane Farenick

Printed in China by Regent Publishing Services Limited

A CIP catalogue record for this book is available from the National Library of Jamaica.

DEDICATION

I wish to dedicate this book to.....
JIMMIE, whose encouragement in the early years laid the groundwork for this book.
ERNEST, whose support and dedication in recent years has helped in making it a reality.
MY CHILDREN....Richard and Beth.
MY SISTERS....Rose and Joyce.
ALL MY FRIENDS... who provided the ingredients for enjoying the food that I cooked as I tried out recipes for this book.

PREFACE

Anyone writing a cook-book has visions of making it different and of being a great help to cooks, both young and old. I present this book for cooks, both new and experienced, foreign and local, passing on the valuable hints I have gathered both here and abroad.

It is written not by a writer who collects recipes, but by a practising Jamaican cook who has used the recipes over the years, altering them for easy cooking, availability of ingredients and noting substitutions when necessary.

But is **this** cook book different? Yes! The simplicity of the recipes allows the cook to make alterations if he or she so desires. I mention **he** because these recipes also are written with the male cook in mind, and in fact all budget-conscious cooks, who have little time to spare and even less time for the kitchen, but who wish to produce tasty, wholesome meals.

When you do live cooking demonstrations in showrooms and on television, as I have done, you have to present recipes that are not only tasty but interesting and different, not to mention time-saving. Working with these recipes for over 30 years, I have become attached to them, and the ease with which they become delicious meals, makes me a happy and satisfied cook.

The wise cook searches for simplicity and there is such a simple pleasure in reading recipes....in allowing the mind to drift over the delightful dishes....the fragrance and flavour in imagination through which a fundamental love of food is awakened.

No other experience can give you that feeling of luxury and graciousness than a well-prepared meal, served on a formal table with appreciative diners. With the right ingredients, company included, it is possible to have this feeling of luxury as often as your budget will allow. Keep the ease of preparation and the short time it took you a secret, but serve the meal with imagination and enjoy it with pleasure.

Cooking is an important part of our culture and should go hand in hand with art and craft and other visible inheritances. Many old Jamaican dishes have been forgotten. Traditional recipes are therefore included for those who would like to recapture childhood memories. If you have never tried them before, now is the time.

I hope readers will benefit from the years of experience of this happy cook, that you will enjoy these recipes as I have done and that this will be your favourite cook-book wherever and whenever you may choose to use it.

JAMAICAN CUISINE
An Introduction

It really was not so long ago that baked products were produced in a brick oven and most meals were cooked on an old-time coal stove. The products were delicious and even though modern methods are slightly more up-to-date, the present-day Jamaican culinary experience is no less exciting to the palate.

Jamaica's culinary history began a long time before the days of coal stoves and brick ovens, and its evolution reflects the history of the island. In fact, it could quite aptly be described as 'out of many one pot'.

To start at the very beginning we should talk about the 'barbacoa' - a wooden grate standing on four forked sticks placed over a slow fire - on which the original inhabitants of the island, the Arawak Indians, spit-roasted fish and meat. This was the forerunner of the present-day barbecue grill, and the cured or cooked meat has now become Jamaica's favourite and famous 'jerk' - chicken, pork, fish, sausage.

This was not all the Arawaks contributed to Jamaican cuisine. They also kept a stock pot in which meat, fish and vegetables which they grew were collected for soup. Saturday beef soup is still a must in most Jamaican households, with the 'leggins' (the necessary vegetables and seasonings) sometimes still sold tied in bundles by market vendors for the convenience of the soup pot.

The other principal foods of the Arawaks were cassava (from which they made bread), corn, sweet potatoes, callaloo, beans, guavas, pineapples, papayas, (more commonly called pawpaw by Jamaicans), fish, conies, iguanas and crabs.

The Arawaks have not been the only influence on Jamaican cuisine. The culinary preferences of other 'people who came' - the Spanish and the British, both of whom controlled the island at one time or another for over five centuries, the Africans who were brought to the island as slaves, the Indians, Jews, Chinese and other Caribbean islanders amongst others - have all helped to create the unique culinary blend which is Jamaican.

Although the Spanish came to Jamaica in 1494, it was not until 150 years later that they brought cattle, goats, pigs, horses and lard from animal fat to the island. They also introduced trees and fruits, such as citrus from Spain (Seville and Valencia oranges), lemon, lime, tamarind, ginger, date palm, pomegranate, plantain, coconuts, grapes, figs, sugar and bananas. Some dishes which are still popular today, such as escoveitched fish, and many peas and bean dishes originated in Spain.

The English controlled the island from 1655 until independence in 1962. They built their kingdom on sugar cultivated by African labour. They also exported rum and molasses which were traded in exchange for flour, pork and pickled fish which were supplied to the slaves and became staples in their diet, and for which Jamaicans still have a great taste today. The English introduced breadfruit, otaheiti apples, ackee, mangoes, rose apples, mandarin, oranges, cherimoyer, tumeric, black pepper and coffee.

In 18th century Jamaica there was no one as rich as an English planter. The lifestyle in the Great Houses in which they lived was lavish, with massive banquet-style feasts being enjoyed on a regular basis as a way of entertaining themselves and visitors. The, Great House cooks would go to market early, and bring back the best there was to offer in fresh fruit and vegetables. Porters or 'boys' would run behind them carrying fare for the stockpot, such as sweet potatoes, yams, dasheen, meat and fish.

Many English dishes and sweets still remain in the Jamaican diet today including roast beef, corned or salt beef, Christmas pudding, Easter bun, pies, tarts, jams and marmalades. The Jamaican fondness for porridge is thought to be a legacy of the Scots.

The Africans, in their turn, created dishes which blended their African traditional food with what was made available to them by their masters. The plantation owners, by law, had to supply their slaves with salted meats at least once a year, and this the slaves supplemented with food which they grew on land for this purpose. Duckunoo and fufu, both of African origin, are still prepared in Jamaican country villages and some of our present day combinations such as ackee and saltfish, mackerel and bananas, called 'rundown', are inventions of African peasants.

The Indians and Chinese, who were brought to the island as indentured labourers after the abolition of slavery, brought their culinary traditions along with them and some survive today. One of Jamaica's favourites, Curry Goat, was introduced by the Indians, and Chinese food is popular amongst the whole population, with Chinese vegetables such as pak choy and mustard being a common sight in supermarkets and markets.

Any description of Jamaican cuisine must focus on its two most popular 'exports' - the hot and spicy jerk cooking and the world famous Blue Mountain coffee. Although much of Jamaican cooking is hot and spicy, no aspect of the local cuisine has captured the taste and talents of visitors as much as the jerk, which has been transformed from a simple road-side fare into a favourite on hotel menus, in private homes and on the streets of New York, Atlanta and California.

Jamaican Blue Mountain Coffee gets its name from the fact that the genuine article is grown in the cradle of the Blue Mountains, which rise to a height of over 7000 feet. It is the island's combination of topography, geology and climate which combine to create the conditions for producing one of the world's best coffees. Through careful monitoring and strict quality control, Jamaica's Blue Mountain coffee continues to maintain its reputation as the peak of perfection and the choice of true connoisseures the world over.

In recent years, Jamaicans seemed to have re-discovered their culinary heritage and adapted many traditional recipes to accommodate the varying tastes of the new generation at home and abroad, as well as visitors to the island who themselves having been captivated by the culinary experience, return home to experiment in their own environment. A few years ago it was a rarity to find any Jamaican dish on a hotel menu and just as difficult to find quality restaurants which specialized in Jamaican cuisine. Today jerk chicken and jerk pork, sit easily beside chicken kiev or roast leg of pork on hotel menus, and callaloo and saltfish are served as an alternative to eggs or pancakes for breakfast on Air Jamaica, the national airline. And if you can't be in Jamaica to enjoy it, many of the ingredients which go into making some of the most popular dishes are available on both sides of the Atlantic, freshly exported from Jamaica or, for the less discriminating, in canned form under a variety of labels.

The story could continue, but on Jamaican tables today is the evidence of its mixed and varied history, this through the variety of fruits, vegetables and prepared dishes, some taken straight from the cuisine of other countries and others adapted by creative Jamaican cooks.

A-Z of Jamaican Foods

This listing of Jamaican foods is by no means comprehensive but will introduce you to some of the island's best-loved fruits, vegetables and dishes. Some you may discover in your grocery store and in the market, while others you may learn about from your Jamaican neighbour.

Ackee [A-ki]

Ackee is a tree vegetable. It is referred to as a fruit that has to be cooked. The tree can be 25 feet high and stands out with its light green leaves. Before the fruit is fully developed, the pods, the size of a medium closed fist, are peach-coloured and tightly closed. They mature to bright red and open to expose the edible portion of three or four sections of golden flesh topped by glossy black seeds. To prepare, these sections are cleaned of their red lining and the seed discarded. The golden flesh is washed, boiled in water or sauteed in oil before joining its accompaniments, salted codfish, tomatoes, onions, escallion and pepper for Jamaica's national dish, ackee and saltfish. When cooked, ackee resembles scrambled egg and most people think the taste is similar.

Allspice (see pimento)

Annatto

This is used as a substitute for saffron or tumeric. It is a deep orange-red, and is used to colour, among other things, Jamaican patties and Stamp and Go (see p. 16) The dried seeds are usually stored in oil.

Bammy [Ba mi]

A round flat bread made from grated cassava (a tuber). Its size varies from wafer thin to 1 inch thick. The thicker size is usually soaked in milk, coconut milk or warm water, before being fried, grilled or steamed and served with fried or escoveitched fish, as well as ackee and saltfish, with avocado as an accompaniment.

Bananas

Green banana used to be looked upon only as an export crop. During World War II Jamaicans had to eat green bananas instead of imported rice. Only then did cooks start experimenting with the green banana calling it 'long grain rice'. The edible banana grows to a height of 10 meters and bears one stem usually consisting of 50-200 fingers weighing about 40-84 kilos.

The banana is a versatile fruit; it can be used ripe as the first fruit in the morning or grilled with bacon on toast. Fresh or dried, green bananas make enjoyable porridge. Boiled green bananas teamed with Rundown, pickled fish or meat cooked in coconut milk, make an excellent lunch or grated and mixed with flour for dumplings. Baked ripe banana with coconut cream is a delicious desert.

Bitter Wood

A tree with a bitter bark used to stimulate appetite and cure fever. The chips are exported for oil and used in the making of tonic water. Old Jamaicans have an enviable knowledge of roots, bark, branches and leaves with funny-sounding names and equally unbelievable uses. They feel the more bitter the medicine, the better the cure.

Breadfruit

The name intrigues most people who do not know the fruit. It was Captain Bligh, on his second voyage to Jamaica in 1793, who brought some 350 breadfruit trees which were planted in the Hope Botanical Gardens in Kingston, and government botanical gardens in the other parishes.

Intended to provide a supply of cheap food for slaves, it was unpopular, and for the first 50 years was fed to pigs. The attractive trees which last a long time need very little care. Their light-green, broad indented leaves, resemble large fingers. Hurricane Gilbert in 1988 uprooted many trees but 2-3 years later they were bearing again and supplying young fruits for boiling in soups and mature ones for stuffing, roasting or baking. They can be made into puddings, drinks, wines, chips and flour or used as you would potato, in salads, etc. Even the blossoms or swords that fall from the trees can be made into a tasty preserve. Yellow heart, a tasty variety grown in the parish of Portland, is much sought after.

Bulla [Bu la]

A round, flat cake made from flour and dark sugar (similar to a Bostonian's Joe Frogger). Its shelf life is long and its traditional partner is avocado (pear). It is a welcome snack at any time for most Jamaicans.

Bustamante Backbone ['Busta']

A tough sweet made from grated coconut and wet sugar. The late Sir Alexander Bustamante, one of our National Heroes and first Prime Minister, was known for his firmness of character, hence the name of the sweet.

Callaloo [Ca-la-lu]

A vegetable closely resembling spinach in appearance and flavour. It is the main ingredient in the popular pepperpot soup. Sauteed with onions and tomatoes, it is a favourite breakfast dish. It is frequently used as a filling in Jamaican vegetable patties, quiches and for fritters.

Cane Vinegar

Made from cane juice, this is the vinegar Jamaicans know and use most... for escoveitched dishes, preserving and pickling, in the treatment of bee and wasp stings, dandruff, douches and for fever when ice is not available.

It is also used on antique furniture to take off grease spots before polishing.

Cassava (also known as manioc)

From cassava we have bammies, farina and cassava meal, puddings, cakes and dumplings. It has been identified as one of the staple foods of the Arawaks, the other being corn. In Jamaica there are sweet and bitter varieties; the sweet is eaten as yam or potato but the bitter is grated, the juice expressed and the starch extracted from the juice to give a good finish to cotton clothes and table linen. In Guyana, Casareep, a sauce not unlike Soya, made from cassava, is used to make Guyanese pepperpot. Cassava pie is made in Bermuda.

Cerassee [Sir-ru-si]

A member of the pumpkin family, the leaves of the plant are used for making a 'tea'. The tea is quite bitter but it is used by many pregnant Jamaican women who feel it is very good for the unborn child's skin. Others feel it's a cure for all manner of ills, including diabetes.

Chew Stick

A bitter stick cut out from the chew stick vine. Long ago the end of the stick was chewed to form a brush and used for cleaning teeth. Some people still use it in making ginger beer but it has largely been replaced by yeast and cream of tartar.

Chocho

Also known as *christophine* or *chayote*. A member of the squash family, it is considered a must in beef soup, as a garnish for escoveitched fish and essential for pickles. It is usually boiled and served hot with butter or grated cheese but blends well with sugar and spice for a pie filling (as mock apple). Chocho grows on a luxuriant vine, resembles a large pear and can be green or white in colour.

Coconut

Jamaicans use coconut in many dishes, the water, the milk, young jelly and hard flesh. Green coconuts yield coconut water, high in potassium. Coconut milk, the white juice from dried coconut, is used in cooking our 'Jamaican Coat of Arms' rice and peas (kidney beans), mackerel Rundown, curried dishes and many other Jamaican favourites. Coconut oil, the base of Jamaican cookery up to two decades ago, is made from coconut milk. A tasty cream is made from coconut milk, and is served with baked bananas and coffee. Copra, a by-product of coconut, makes soap. The fibrous coir of the dry coconut husk was used for mattresses, but is now an integral part of the potting soil for our beautiful anthurium, and other potted plants. The coconut tree has many uses. In earlier times, and sometimes even today, the long shiny leaves were plaited to make a welcome arch for weddings. The spear of the leaves are stripped and used to string the hibiscus petal in vases, forming a welcome bouquet in many Jamaican hotel foyers. The mesh on the base of the tree can be used as a strainer. Immature coconuts were (and sometimes still are) used to clean beautiful wooden floors and some dried nuts are made into ornaments which are sold in craft shops and along roadsides.

The shell of the dry coconut is used for fuel or as a container for attractive dishes.

Duckunoo [Du-ku-nu] (or Tie-a-Leaf)

A pudding made from cornmeal or green bananas, coconut, sugar and spices. It used to be wrapped in green banana leaf, tied with banana string and steamed. The dark blue colouring imparted by the banana leaf and the shape of the fold have given rise to duckunoos' popular name 'Blue Drawers'.

Escallion and Thyme

Escallion is Jamaica's most popular seasoning for nearly all savoury dishes. It grows well in the parish of St. Elizabeth with very little rainfall, using plenty of dried grass as mulch. Escallion, planted in a bed of roses, is supposed to keep insects away. It is now being used a lot for garnishing when cut as confetti, or as stems for vegetable flowers. Thyme, a shrubbery plant, is usually sold with escallion since most dishes use escallion and thyme for enhancement.

Escoveitched Fish [Eskoveech Fish]

Freshly-caught fish, seasoned and fried, is left in a sauce of vinegar, onions, chocho, carrots and pepper for hours or overnight, since this is a popular breakfast dish. It is similar to *ceviche* except that the fish is fried. This is quite likely born out of the need to keep the fish from spoiling until ready for use.

BREADFRUIT
SOURSOP
NASEBERRY
ORTANIQUE
PIMENTO
BANANA
GINGER
CHOCHO
UGLI

MANGO

GUINEP

JUNE PLUM

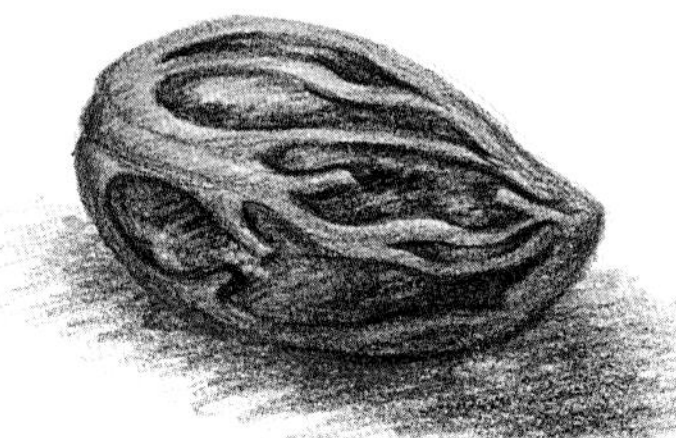

NUTMEG

PAW-PAW

COCONUT

LIGNUM VITAE

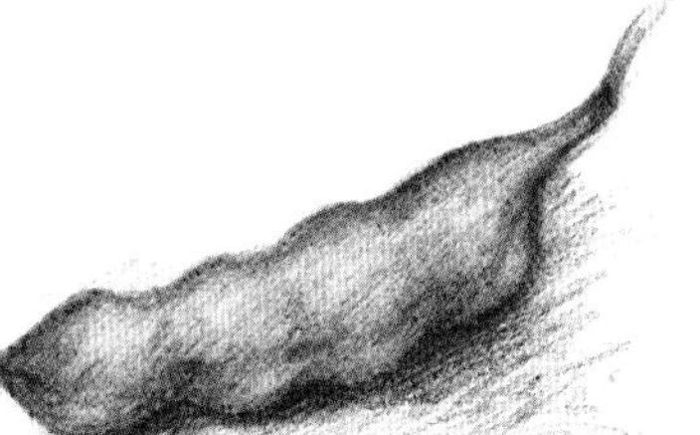

TAMARIND

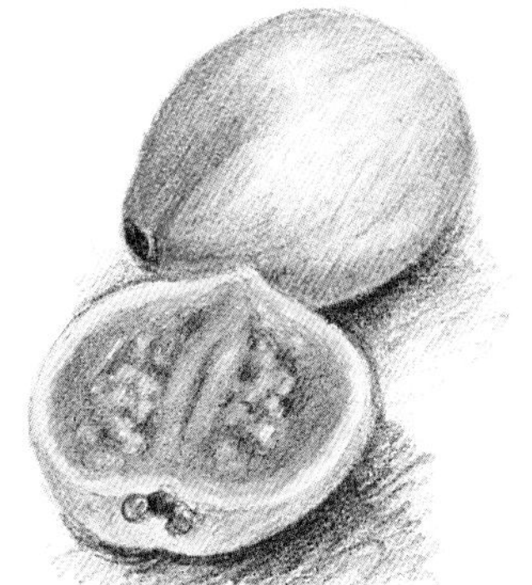

GUAVA

Festival

A dumpling made with cornmeal, flour, salt and sugar and then fried. It is similar to a 'hush puppy' and shaped like a thin hot dog roll. Frequently served with 'jerk' dishes.

Fish Tea

A broth made by boiling fish, usually heads and tails, and any available vegetables except beetroot. It is highly seasoned with allspice, salt and pepper and served steaming hot.

Ginger

A favourite of the Chinese community, ginger came to us from the Far East around 1527. Jamaican ginger has a special flavour and is used for ginger beer, candies and cookies as well as with meat, poultry, fish and vegetables. Hot ginger 'tea' is widely used as a home remedy for an upset stomach.

Guava

There are two kinds of guavas in Jamaica, a round, yellow fruit called common guava with plenty of pectin and used for jellies, jams and toppings, and a pear-shaped guava called Spanish Guava, eaten fresh, stewed or used in pies. Both are good sources of vitamin C. Guavas are highly perfumed and when cut across reveal pale yellow or bright pink flesh with a mass of seeds inside.

Guinep

Called Jamaica's lychee, it is a small green fruit that bears in clusters rather like grapes. It has a leathery outer skin and a large seed with a covering of tangy-sweet pulp.

Herbs (and Spices)

Mention herb in Jamaica and you may be asked if you mean the weed ganja, (otherwise called Marijuana). Jamaican ganja is of a high quality but its possession, use or sale is illegal and could land you in jail and remember there are no gourmet meals there.

What's the difference between a herb and a spice?

A herb is a seed plant whose stem does not develop woody tissue as that of a shrub or tree but persists only long enough for the development of flowers and seeds. Herbs are annual, biennial or perennial, according to the length of life of their roots. The average Jamaican uses herbs more for healing than for flavouring. A spice is a plant of economic value, used for medicinal purposes and for its sweet scent or flavour. A spice is that which enriches or alters the taste of food - that which gives zest or pungency and a piquant or pleasing flavour.

Irish Moss

A variety of seaweed which when cleaned, dried and boiled, yields a gelatinous cream-coloured liquid. It is sweetened with condensed milk and flavoured with nutmeg and vanilla. A popular drink with health food enthusiasts, Irish Moss is believed to aid sexual prowess.

Janga

A river crayfish that makes a delicious soup. Jangas are usually small but can grow to quite a large size.

Jerk

A highly-seasoned barbecued dish cooked on smouldering pimento wood over a small pit. The maroons jerked wild pigs in Portland while on the run from the British. Jerk has been a part of our culinary tradition for centuries. Now we not only jerk pork, but chicken, fish - in fact all meats.

Johnny Cake

These fried dumplings were originally called 'journey cakes' as they would be packed in the lunch pails of the plantation workers, for a long lasting and hearty snack. Johnny cakes are often served at breakfast as a bread substitute. A dough mixture is shaped into medium-sized balls and fried in hot oil. They may be used as a substitute for baking powder biscuits.

June Plum

At times called Jew plum, (or Golden Apple in other Caribbean islands) it is a tangy, oval-shaped fruit with green skin which turns yellow when ripe. The large seed which has spiky protuberances, is a good source of Vitamin C. June plum may be eaten fresh or stewed with sugar and spices or made into a drink.

Kola nut

Known as '*bissy*', it is said to contain more caffeine than coffee berries. The nut is dried and stored in an airtight container and used for mild stomach upsets and diarrhoea. It is considered by old time Jamaicans to be an antidote for some poisons.

Leggings

This bundle of pumpkin, cabbage, carrot, turnip and parsley used to be sold in quantities needed to make beef soup on Saturdays for 4-6 persons. This packaging of 'legumes' was done by higglers years ago for the convenience of the soup pot.

Lignum Vitae

The National Flower of Jamaica. This plant takes years to grow into a large tree. It produces beautiful clusters of powder blue blooms. The many toned wood is used to produce much sought after furniture, cutting boards, cheese boards and salad bowls for the elegant table. Although during the summer months butterflies are attracted to the tree, during the rest of the year the branches are used in kitchens and pantries to keep flies away.

The National tree is the Blue Mahoe.

Lime

More popular in Jamaica than lemons, they are used in Jamaican-style lemonade. Made with dark-brown sugar, the mixture is sometimes called wash. It is also served with other exotic drinks and in wedges as a garnish for fresh fish.

Mango

A popular bright yellow fruit available in a number of sizes and varieties. The skin is greenish yellow when ripe. Green mangoes are used in chutney, a preferred accompaniment to curried dishes. They are used ripe in fruit salad while the juice combines well in a fruit punch. Among the most popular mangoes are Bombay, East Indian, St. Julian, Nelson, Tommy Atkins and Robin.

Mannish Water

A thick, highly-seasoned soup made from goat offal, green bananas, and any available vegetables or tubers. Believed to be a tonic, it is an important dish at country weddings and other festive occasions when curried goat is served as one of the main entrees.

Matrimony

This is not only an arranged marriage, after being resident in Jamaica for only 24 hours, but it is also a fruit salad made from star apples, a succulent purple or green fruit, with orange, grapefruit and condensed milk.

Naseberry [Nees berry]

Also called *sapodilla*, naseberry is a russet-brown fruit about the size of a peach. It has a thin edible skin with a pale brown, sweet and delicately-flavoured pulp. It looks like a Kiwi fruit. Although grown islandwide it flourishes along the south and east coasts. Naseberries are best eaten fresh or added to fruit salad.

Nutmeg

This plant, described by an ancient writer as a tree with perfume of two kinds, grows to a height of 15 to 30 feet and the nut is well protected. It is a remarkable tree producing two different spices, nutmeg and mace. Its fleshy fruit called nutmeg peri-carp resembles an apricot and is pale yellow in colour. When mature and still attached to its branch, it splits in two as if by magic, exposing a beautiful, brilliant, scarlet, netlike membrane known as mace which snugly encases a shiny, dark, brittle shell. This shell encloses the single, pale brown, oily seed, the nutmeg. Jamaican housewives prefer to keep their nutmeg in this shell until they are ready to use it. Then it is freshly grated on a special small nutmeg grater. It is used in eggnog, custards, buns, porridge, milk, quiches and to enchance coconut dishes.

Ortanique [or ta neek]

A unique fruit developed by Jamaican agronomists, it is a cross between the orange and the tangerine. The juice is a rich golden colour with a unique flavour.

Otaheite apple

A sweet pear-shaped fruit resembling the shape of the tree. Deep, burgundy-red on the outside, milk white on the inside, it has a large brown seed and a delicate flavour. Dark- red skins seem to have more flavour than burgundy ones. The slightly underripe fruit when stewed makes a delicious pie.

Patty

A delicious crescent-shaped meat pie made with highly seasoned minced meat, lobster, shrimps, chicken or vegetables into a flaky pastry shell. Very popular as a snack, the patty is Jamaica's No.1 fast food. Popular lunch is a patty or two with an ice cold soft drink.

Paw-paw [pa-pah]

Also known as papaya, the fruit is yellow or orange when ripe and is a good source of vitamin A. The young fruits are used in stews and the leaves are used as meat tenderizer. It is said the papain is extracted and used in commercial tenderizer. Jamaicans do not plant the trees near the house or tie animals near to the tree as it is supposed to make people or animals weak and infertile.

Pear

Known as avocado to everyone else except Jamaicans!

Pimento

Known in North America as allspice, it is not to be confused with pimento, the pepper. It is called allspice because the flavour is a blend of cinnamon, nutmeg, mace and cloves and is used in sweet as well as savoury dishes. In appearance it is just like peppercorns and grows on a tall sturdy tree. The ripe purple seeds are used to make a pimento liqueur and is also used to enliven Benedictine and Chartreuse. The leaves and the wood are used in the cooking of jerk dishes and the berries powdered to season the meat. Jamaica supplies about 80% of the world's consumption of allspice. Used by the Russians in the production of sausages, it is also used in soups, pickles, marinades, pies and fish dishes. It helps in the preserving of food.

Plantain

A cousin of the banana that has to be cooked. Delicious when ripe, fried, baked, candied, or fried green, crushed and salted, or made into plantain chips.

Pone

A compact pudding made from cornmeal flour, sugar, coconut milk and spices. The texture is much harder than pudding.

Potatoes (sweet)

Sweet potatoes are baked, roasted, made into souffles or puddings or fried and served with pork. Sweet potatoes come in a variety of colours; yellow, cream, white and light orange. Some people prefer the white sweet potatoes for puddings but all can be used.

Rundown

Salted mackerel, shad or codfish simmered in coconut milk that has been boiled to a custard along with tomatoes, onions, escallion and pepper. Boiled green bananas usually accompany this dish.

Scotch Bonnet

One of the hottest peppers, shaped like a Scotsman's bonnet. It is used in most Jamaican dishes for its special flavour. Green scotch bonnet peppers are used to give flavour to soups. The peppers are carefully taken out before they burst, to impart their hot flavour. We do have small peppers called 'bird peppers' used by the Indian population for some of their dishes, and for pepper flavoured wine, but scotch bonnet is the preferred pepper.

Sorrel

The favourite drink of Jamaicans at Christmas time. The drink is made from the sorrel plant, a low bushy shrub with red stems and calices which comes into 'season' towards the end of the year. No Jamaican Christmas is complete without bottles of the red drink brewed with rum and ginger.

Soursop

A large green-skinned fruit with a spiky, rough textured coat and cottony white pulp. The flavour is an interesting mix of sour and sweet. It can be sweetened with condensed milk and nutmeg, but is more refreshing with sugar and lime, and makes a delicious ice cream.

Sweet Pepper

Because we use so much pepper, green pepper is called Sweet Pepper, and is used to flavour Jamaican pepper steaks and other seasoned rice dishes and one pot meals.

Tamarind [Tam-rine]

An acid tasting fruit that has a brittle brown shell. Inside, fairly large seeds are covered by a tangy brown pulp. Tamarind may be eaten as a fresh fruit, rolled in granulated sugar to produce a candy (tamarind balls) or mixed with water and sugar to yield a delightful summer drink. The leaves are used to make a drink for patients with measles, and the Chinese use it in their sweet and sour dishes.

Ugli

A citrus fruit like the ortanique developed by Jamaican agronomists. The flavour and texture is somewhat similar to grapefruit. It is a cross between an orange and a grapefruit.

Wash

A beverage made from brown sugar, water and lime or sour oranges.

Wet Sugar

Unrefined sugar, deep brown and moist produced by boiling cane juice until it crystallizes. Unlike refined sugar it contains all the rich nutrients found in cane juice. The molasses is said to be good for the nerves.

Yams

There are many varieties of yams. White yam as the name implies is white and often dried and kept for a long period. Taw is a cross between yellow and white yam. Lucea yam is whitish in colour. Renta or Barbados yam and Sweet yam are soft yams. Hard yam is hard and white. St. Vincent is a soft yam with a thin purple layer under the skin. Yampie [yampi] a small delicate flavoured white African tuber often served boiled or roasted. The Africans contributed a lot to the Jamaican cuisine. Not allowed fresh meat they developed tasty meals with pickled meat and fish, ochroes and yam.

Zest

This is easy to find on our thinly peeled citrus or what you feel when you down a drink of our famous Jamaican Rum.

FOR STARTERS

Some of our appetizers and hors d'oeuvres are so tasty you can easily eat enough of them and only realize when you have breasted the tape that they were just starters and not the main course.

Pick the start with a tasty appetizer, it is important to form first impressions even in the heats.

Coconut starters always jump the gun but they are an unbeatable talking point and unbelievably delicious; in fact any of our vegetables such as callaloo in a fritter batter, carefully fried, will quickly disappear before nodding heads and opened mouths. Bananas, breadfruit, ackees, eggs and jerk sausages used in imaginative ways are easy on the pocket and palate.

Saltfish used innovatively, as well as crab backs, make tasty titbits, not to mention pepper shrimps which have their own corner at Middle Quarters, in the parish of St. Elizabeth. Whereas the name of the corner may escape your memory, the taste of the shrimps will be enshrined in your culinary archives.

How many hors d'oeuvres to serve is always a dilemma but three cold ones, two hot ones and a selection of cheeses and crackers with a platter of raw, cold vegetables (crudites), with a choice of dips is usually enough. Hors d'oeuvres should be small enough to be easily eaten in one or two bites and cold ones should be served before hot ones.

Curried Ackees in Bread Cups (front)
Codfish Fritters (back)
Breadfruit Chips

Curried Ackees
(in bread cups)

6	*ackees (pods)*
1 cup	*coconut milk*
½ tsp.	*salt*
½ tsp.	*lime juice*
1 tsp.	*chutney or hot sauce*
2 tbsp.	*flour*
1 tbsp.	*curry powder*
2 tbsp.	*butter or oil*
1	*onion*
1	*red pepper*

1. Wash and prepare ackees for cooking, by taking the pods from the shell, discarding the black seeds, and taking out the pink lining from the flesh of the ackee.
2. Cook for 5 minutes in boiling, salted water. Drain ackees and set aside.
3. Heat oil and add curry powder and cook on slow heat.
4. Add all ingredients except ackees, and bring to the boil and skim.
5. Lower heat and cook until the crude taste of the curry has disappeared.
6. Add ackees, cook on very gentle flame, until ackees are tender but whole, and the sauce is absorbed.
7. When ready to serve, pile on toasted cassava wafers, crisp toasted rounds, or in bread cups.

Yields 6 servings.

Bread cups are easy to make:

6	*slices day-old bread*

1. Cut crust from day-old slices.
2. Use rolling pin to flatten slices.
3. Press into muffin pans to shape.
4. Bake at 350° F approx. for 10 minutes or until cups are toasted and stay in shape.
5. Remove from muffin tin and allow to cool.
6. Do not fill until just before serving.
7. Fill with curried ackees, chicken *a la king* and other tasty fillings.

Bacon Bows

6	*slices of day-old bread*
6	*pieces cheese, ½ inch square by 3 inches long*
6	*slices streaky bacon, or 3 slices cut in half*

1. Use a rolling pin and roll bread slices until flattened.
2. Wrap 1 piece cheese in 1 slice bread. Cut in half and tie with bacon, or fasten with a toothpick.
3. Put on a greased sheet.
4. When ready to serve, bake or grill until bacon is cooked.
5. Serve hot.

Yields 12.

Jerk Sausage in Bacon Blanket

6	*jerk sausages*
½ lb.	*bacon*

1 Cut each sausage into 3 pieces.

2 Wrap sausage pieces in bacon and fasten with a toothpick.

3 When ready to serve, bake or grill for about 10 minutes.

4 Serve hot.

Yields 18

Cook's Tip

When serving; it is advisable to leave some pieces without the bacon blanket for those guests who would prefer not to have bacon.

Coco Fritters

In these days of scarce and expensive salted cod try this for taste - it's good!

1 cup	*chopped raw coco*
1	*small onion*
1 tsp.	*baking powder*
2	*tbsp. evaporated milk*
2	*stalks escallion*
	salt and pepper to taste
	vegetable oil for deep frying

1 Put all ingredients in blender and blend until smooth.

2 Drop by tbsp. into deep fat and fry.

3 Drain and serve hot.

Yields 10

Callaloo Fritters

2 cups	*raw callaloo cut up*
½	*an onion*
1	*tomato*
1 tbsp.	*margerine*

Batter:

1⅓ cups	*all purpose flour*
¼ tsp.	*salt (optional)*
1 tsp.	*baking powder*
1	*egg*
	vegetable oil for deep frying

1 Heat margerine, saute onion and tomato.

2 Add callaloo and steam for about 5-10 minutes.

3 Cool and set aside.

4 Sift flour, measure, sift again with baking powder and salt.

5 Beat egg and add to cooked callaloo.

6 Combine egg and callaloo with flour mixture.

7 Heat frying pan and add oil to a depth of ½ inch.

8 Drop by tbsp., in hot oil and fry.

9 Serve hot.

Yields 12.

Codfish Fritters

(Stamp and Go)

This popular Jamaican fritter can be served for breakfast or as an hors d'oeuvre with cocktails. It is said to be one of, or the only thing that the late Jamaican National Hero, the Rt. Honourable Norman Washington Manley, had at cocktail parties.

½ lb.	*salted codfish*
½ lb.	*flour*
2	*onions*
2	*tomatoes (plummy)*
2	*cloves garlic*
½	*hot pepper - scotch bonnet if possible*
2	*stalks escallion*
2 tbsp.	*oil*
2 tsp.	*baking powder*
	oil for frying

1 Soak codfish, preferably overnight. Drain, rinse under cold water, flake the fish, making sure to remove fish bones.

2 Chop finely, tomatoes, onion, garlic, escallion and pepper.

3 Saute in 2 tbsp. oil. Drain off oil and cool.

4 Add seasoning to raw codfish. Set aside.

5 Add baking powder to flour. Add codfish to flour.

6 Add enough water to make a medium batter.

7 Fry by tbsp. in about ½ inch of oil or deep fat until golden brown.

8 Drain on absorbent paper.

9 Serve hot.

Yields 24

Codfish Balls

These are softer than codfish fritters, and are usually served with a cocktail sauce.

½ lb.	*salted codfish*
2 cups	*diced, raw potatoes*
1 tbsp.	*butter*
½ tsp.	*pepper*
2	*eggs, beaten*
	bread crumbs
	vegetable oil for deep frying

1 Soak codfish in water, preferably overnight. Boil for ½ hour. Drain, rinse under cold water and flake the fish making sure to remove fine bones.

2 Boil diced potatoes for 20 minutes.

3 Add butter, pepper and shredded fish to potatoes , mix well.

4 Form mixture into light, feathery balls. Dip in beaten egg then breadcrumbs.

5 Fry in deep oil in fryer basket until golden brown.

6 Drain on absorbent paper and serve very hot with a cocktail sauce.

Yields 12

Crab Backs (front)
Callaloo Fritters
Pepper Shrimps (back)

Crab Backs

During the May rainy season many people go out to hunt for land crabs. This delicacy is generally cooked in a big kerosene pan...... yes, you guessed it, kerosene oil came in it originally, and the empty pan is now used for boiling white clothes, cooking curried goat, and boiling crabs, often on an open fire. Green bananas, salt and other seasonings are added to the pot for this feast.

George and Myrtle Murray come to mind as soon as I think of boiled crabs.

12	*crabs*
6	*slices of bread*
1 cup	*milk*
2 oz.	*butter*
1	*onion, finely chopped*
6 oz.	*bread crumbs*
	salt and black pepper to taste.

1 Clean crabs thoroughly, removing stomach etc. Drop crabs in boiling water and boil for 10 minutes approximately. Remove claws and extract all the meat from the crabs and claws. Clean and reserve crab back shells.

2 In the meantime, soak bread in milk.

3 Preheat oven to 400° F.

4 Chop crab meat finely.

5 Mix soaked bread with chopped onion, black pepper, salt and crab meat.

6 Pack crab meat mixture into clean, empty crab shells, sprinkle with bread crumbs and dot with butter.

7 Bake for 15-20 minutes on top shelf of hot oven (400° F).

8 Serve hot.

Yields 6

Pepper Shrimp

This is a hot spicy appetizer.

5 lb.	*shrimps thawed and rinsed (left in shells)*
1 cup	*salad oil*
2	*cloves garlic*
2 tsp.	*salt*
2	*scotch bonnet peppers or 6 Bird peppers*
2 tbsp.	*vinegar*

1 In a heavy dutch oven, put oil, garlic, salt and pepper to heat.

2 Add shrimps and stir for 5 minutes.

3 Sprinkle on vinegar and cook for a further 5 minutes.

Serves 6-8

Cook's Tip

5 pints of water may be used instead of oil - boil everything together, except shrimps, for 10 minutes. Add shrimps and cook for 10 minutes more.

Cocktail Patties

Patties are Jamaica's favourite fast food. At lunch time patty outlets are crowded, and this popular meat pie certainly holds its own at cocktail parties. If you haven't made patties before, I suggest you start with the cocktail size.

Our patties are like cornish pasties, and the pastry can be filled with beef which is the most popular filling or chicken, lobster, shrimp, and callaloo or mixed vegetables.

The original Jamaican patty crust is made with beef suet, but a short crust pastry can be used.

Pastry:

1 lb.	*flour*
1 tsp.	*baking powder*
1 tsp.	*salt*
½ cup	*ground beef suet*
½ cup	*vegetable shortening*
8 oz.	*iced water (approx.)*
	a pinch of tomato colouring in water, or
	a drop annatto colouring to colour pastry

Filling:

1 lb.	*ground beef*
2	*stalks escallion*
1	*stalk thyme (about ½ teaspoon dried thyme)*
1	*medium onion*
2 cups	*bread crumbs*
½ tsp.	*pepper*
1 tsp.	*salt*
1 tsp.	*sugar*
	browning (optional)
	butter
	oil for glazing

To make pastry:

1 Sift the flour and salt.

2 Mix the suet and vegetable shortening with some of the flour.

3 Mix suet mixture and remaining flour, and add baking powder.

4 Add water with colouring and mix until the ingredients are bound together and leave the basin clean. The dough should be firm.

5 Turn on to a floured board. Knead till free from cracks.

6 Divide dough into 40 pieces and shape into balls.

7 Cover and leave until ready to make patties.

To make filling:

1 Heat mince meat in a saucepan with just enough water to cover.

2 Use fingers or fork to separate lumps in the water.

3 Add seasoning, finely chopped, to meat and also ½ tsp. salt and sugar.

4 Cook until mince is soft, about 30 minutes on low heat.

5 Correct seasoning and add remaining salt.

6 Add bread crumbs and browning if a darker colouring is required.

7 Make sure there is enough gravy to make filling wet. Add butter, and allow to cool before putting into pastry.

8 Preheat oven to 350° F.

9 On a lightly floured board, roll out balls in circles. Put about 1 full teaspoon of mince in centre of circles and fold over to form a crescent. Press together and crimp with a crimper or a fork, brushing a little oil on each patty.

10 Bake for approximately 45 minutes until golden brown or deep fry cocktail patties.

11 Serve hot.

Yields 40 cocktail size patties.

Coconut Chips

1	*dry coconut*
	salt

1 After removing the flesh from the shell of the coconut, pare off the brown skin, and cut in strips about ¼ inch thick.

2 Wash and drain.

3 Bake in a moderate oven (350°F) on a greased tin sheet until lightly browned. (Do not over brown.)

4 Sprinkle with salt. Serve as you would nuts.

Yields 8 servings.

Breadfruit Chips

1	*breadfruit*
1 tsp.	*salt*
	enough water to cover chips
	vegetable oil for deep frying

1 Select a firm fit breadfruit.

2 Peel and remove heart.

3 Cut into thin slices, and stand in salted water.

4 Drain and dry chips.

5 Fry in deep, hot oil until crisp, but not brown.

6 Serve hot or cold.

Yields 24 thin slices (which is never enough for Jamaicans)

Solomon Gundy

Good to serve with Jamaican rum drinks.

Paste:

3 lb.	*red herring (bloaters)*
8 oz.	*onion*
1	*hot pepper (without seeds)*
5 oz.	*vinegar*
2 tbsp.	*oil*
1 tbsp.	*rum*

1 Roast red herring by wrapping in newspaper and lighting until roasted or pour rum on and light.

2 Take bones out of red herring, flake flesh and set flesh aside.

3 Grind flesh with onions and pepper, and mix with other ingredients to make a smooth paste.

Yields enough paste for two 8 oz. jars.

Butter:

1 tsp. Solomon Gundy paste in 2 oz. butter. Mix and put on pita bread or crackers.

Cucumber Cups (front)
Cocktail Patties

Coconut Toast

This was always a very welcome treat and a conversation piece when served at Lady Glasspole's pleasant teas at King's House.

5	*slices of bread*
5 oz.	*condensed milk*
1	*dry coconut*
	pinch of salt (optional)
	pinch of nutmeg (optional)

1 Grate coconut on large cutter. Add pinch of salt and nutmeg to grated coconut if desired and set aside.

2 Cut each slice of bread into 3 fingers each and butter.

3 Pour ½ tin (about 5 oz.) condensed milk in shallow bowl.

4 Dip each finger in the condensed milk and then into the grated coconut. Place on platter.

5 When ready to serve bake at 350° F for 7-10 minutes or until brown.

Yields 15

Pizza Sandwiches

12	*slices bread*
½ cup	*grated Parmesan cheese*
½ lb.	*grated cheddar cheese*
2 cups	*diced, peeled ripe tomatoes, drained*
1	*peeled, minced clove of garlic*
½ tsp.	*salt*
½ tsp.	*pepper*
½ tsp.	*dried oregano*
2 tbsp.	*oil*
1 tbsp.	*fresh basil*
1 tbsp.	*ketchup*

1 Preheat oven to 425° F.

2 Mix all ingredients together except the Parmesan cheese, oil and the bread.

3 Cut slices of bread in rounds or wedges.

4 Put tomato and cheese mixture on bread, sprinkle with Parmesan cheese, brush oil on top and bake for 10-15 minutes.

Yields 12

Festive Cheese Balls

1 cup	*cottage cheese*
8 oz.	*cream cheese softened*
2 oz.	*finely shredded sharp cheddar cheese*
1 oz.	*Roquefort cheese, crumbled*
1	*medium onion, finely grated*
1 tbsp.	*Pickapeppa sauce*
1 tbsp.	*dry or medium sherry*
½ cup	*chopped nuts*
½ cup	*chopped parsley*

1 In a bowl combine first 7 ingredients and mix well.

2 Shape into 2 balls.

3 Roll each ball in nuts, then roll in parsley.

4 Chill thoroughly.

5 Serve with crackers.

Serves 12.

Stuffed Hard-Boiled Eggs

6 eggs

1 Hard boil eggs by putting in cold water to cover, and boil for 20 minutes. As soon as eggs are cooked, remove from heat and put under cold water to cool. (If left in boiling water they will continue to cook and may end up with a dark ring around the yolk.)

2 When ready to shell eggs, tap the shell all around to get rid of the air. Take shell off and rinse. Set aside.

3 Cut hard-boiled eggs into halves lengthwise or crosswise, with knife or crimp cutter.

4 Remove yolks carefully. Wash the white of the egg and drain, fill with the following fillings:

a *Chopped ripe olives and cheese.*

b *Cottage cheese, chives, crisp bacon, mashed egg yolks, parsley, and mayonnaise.*

c *Chopped celery with mayonnaise or French dressing.*

d *Egg yolk, finely chopped pickle and mayonnaise.*

e *Egg yolk and mayonnaise or egg yolk with butter, salt and pepper.*

Yields 12 halves.

Cook's Tip

It is advisable to boil 8 eggs to get 6 well shaped stuffed eggs. It is better to keep the stuffing simple as too many additions mask the real egg taste. Devilled egg is stuffed egg with pepper.

Cucumber Cups

3 cucumbers
1 cup flaked tuna
¼ cup minced sweet pickle
1 tbsp. lemon juice
Salt and black pepper to taste.

1 Cut cucumbers into 2 inch lengths each.

2 Scoop out centres and drain.

3 Mix all other ingredients together.

4 Fill cucumber cups with mixture.

5 Chill and serve garnished with sections of ripe olives, or fill with a filling of your choice.

Yields 6

Banana Hors D'oeuvres

2	*large ripe bananas*
1 cup	*lemon juice*
3 oz.	*cream cheese*
⅓ cup	*chopped nut meats*

1 Peel bananas and cut crosswise into 1 inch pieces.

2 Marinate in lemon juice for 1 hour.

3 Drain, cover with cream cheese, and roll in nut meats.

4 Chill.

Serves 8.

Scotch Eggs

½ lb.	*sausage meat or sausages*
4	*hard-boiled eggs*
1 tbsp.	*seasoned flour*
	a little piquant sauce
	beaten eggs
	bread crumbs
	vegetable oil for deep frying

1 Remove sausage meat from the skins.

2 Shell the eggs and dust lightly with seasoned flour.

3 Crush sausage meat and add a few drops of sauce to the meat. Divide equally into 4.

4 Cover each egg with sausage meat, doing this as evenly as possible to keep the egg in good shape.

5 Brush over with beaten egg, roll in bread crumbs and fry in deep fat.

6 When the eggs are golden brown in colour, remove from fat, drain, cool and then cut in half.

Yields 4.

Pizza Sandwiches (left)
Bacon Bows (right)
Coconut Toast (back)

Baked Eggs on Anchovy Rings

Years ago, before I realized that Dr. Mavis Gilmour was a Cordon Bleu cook, she gave me a Cordon Bleu Cookbook and this recipe on the steps of the Y.W.C.A., when I started a Hostess Club for that Association.

6	*eggs*
6-12	*anchovy fillets*
1	*medium onion*
2	*tomatoes*
	salt
	pepper

1 Preheat oven to 375° F

2 Grease ovenproof custard cups.

3 Add anchovies, sauteed onion rings, tomato wedges, in fact anything you would like with eggs.

4 Break eggs on top, sprinkle with pepper (salt may not be necessary since anchovies are quite salty).

5 Stand cups in baking dish in ½ inch hot water, bake eggs at 375°F. for 15-20 minutes.

6 Serve hot, immediately.

Serves 6.

SATURDAY SOUPS

&

OTHER BROTHS

Old-time Jamaican kitchens had a three-legged iron stock pot that was always ready to boil precious scraps and left-overs daily. Without refrigerators this ensured the making of 'tomorrow soup'.

The stock pot was stored above the fireplace with iron hooks called 'pot hook' and 'hangers' and children at school were taught to write by using these symbols.

Pot hooks and hangers were not the only things that rested on the two parallel iron bars over the fireplace but there was also the 'Kreng Kreng' basket used to smoke and preserve corned pork, smoked tripe, smoked tongue, and other parts of the 'fifth quarter' (see p. 90).

Don't 'dis' soup, however, because of its humble origins. It has graduated with dignity into modern Jamaica and is enjoyed in precious china or sawn off bamboo joints, served at banquets or feeds. As popular as Jamaican rum is, soup is its rival beside the glass at dominoes or poker games, lunch or dinner.

The Christmas ham bone can end up in any of Jamaican soups with the exception of fish tea. It is especially good in red peas (kidney beans), pumpkin, and pepperpot soup made with callaloo.

Although we are a hot island, Jamaicans do not like cold soups, but Mrs. Gloria Smith, a born gourmet, has collected many compliments for cold soups served at her elegant dinners.

Remember all the cook's secrets, like thyme, escallion, green pepper etc. should be removed before the soup is served.

Remember also that a soup should smile, chuckle but never laugh in a full rollicking boil.

FISH CHOWDER

¼ lb.	*salt pork, diced*
3	*medium sliced onions*
1½ lb.	*fish fillets (cut in medium pieces)*
5 lb.	*diced white potatoes*
4 tsp.	*salt*
¼ tsp.	*pepper*
3 cups	*boiling water*
1 qt.	*milk*
1 cup	*evaporated milk*
3 tbsp.	*butter*

1 Fry salt pork in its own fat until crisp and brown. Remove pork bits and set aside.

3 Add onions to pork fat, and cook until tender, stirring occasionally.

4 Add potatoes, salt, pepper and boiling water to onions. Lay fish on top.

5 Cover and simmer for 25 minutes or until potatoes are tender.

6 Pour in evaporated milk. Add butter and pork bits. Heat thoroughly.

Serves 6

Saturday Beef Soup

Saturday soup got its name from the fact that cows were slaughtered on Friday and soup bones would spoil quickly. As a result, the soup was prepared on Saturday along with fresh vegetables from the market and the beef 'goose neck', if the butcher considered you a favourite customer. The soup made was second to none. Saturday was a busy day for all householders since precious little was done on Sunday. The house was thoroughly cleaned, the ice box or refrigerator, defrosted or cleaned, the silver polished, the bed linen changed and all baking and cooking that could be done on Saturday was done. Not to mention, cleaning of shoes, ironing of clothes, packing the press or chest of drawers and washing whatever was exposed on the open wagon. The fresh smell of cleaning agents, and the aroma of home baking permeating the atmosphere, the smell of freshly cut grass and the changing state of readiness for the morrow, made it impossible to do too much more than a one pot soup. Many Jamaicans cannot recognize the day without soup, even though the familiar scenes and scents have vanished.

1 lb.	*soup bones or stewing steak*
½ lb.	*carrots, cubed*
¼ lb.	*turnips, cubed*
1 lb.	*pumpkin, cut up*
½ lb.	*coco, cut up*
1 lb.	*yellow yam, cut up*
½ lb.	*cabbage*
1	*sprig thyme*
2	*stalks escallion*
2 qt.	*water*

1 Boil soup bones in 2 qts. water (about 30 minutes in pressure cooker.)

2 Cut up vegetables, yam and coco and add with seasonings to soup.

3 Dumplings may be added if desired.

4 Once it starts boiling, simmer uncovered until yam is cooked and soup is of a medium consistency.

***Serves* 6**

Fish Tea

Most soups in Jamaica are started from scratch using a well-flavoured stock. Jamaicans like the fish head so this is not set aside to make stock. They prefer to eat the head and use the fillet for soup or they will buy some fish specially for soup or fish tea as it is called. Jamaicans call all hot beverages 'tea' and since fish gives a light stock, it is called tea. Small fish can be used to make a stock.

1 lb.	*fish or fish head and cut into pieces*
2 qt.	*cold water*
1	*medium onion, diced*
1	*clove garlic*
1	*sprig thyme*
2	*stalks escallion*
	celery (optional)
1 lb.	*potatoes, cubed*
1	*green scotch bonnet pepper*

1 Boil fish in water with thyme until flavour is released in water (about 30 minutes). Do not cover the pot.

2 Strain stock and take flesh from fish and set aside.

3 Add remaining ingredients and simmer until potatoes are cooked, about 20 minutes.

4 Return flesh to soup and serve hot.

***Serves* 6**

Cook's Tip

Care must be taken not to over flavour stock and lose the delicate flavour of the tea.

Fish Tea with Corn Bread

Jamaican Pepperpot Soup (callaloo)

The main ingredient in the Jamaican pepperpot soup is callaloo which is of African origin and is teamed with ochroes, kale and other tender heart leaves from the eddoe family (dasheen, badoo, coco etc.). It mixes corned pig's tail, salt beef, ham hock, fresh beef and shrimp (if liked) with vegetables like yam, coco, and dumpling in a broth. Spicy flavourings like pimento, thyme, garlic, escallion and green scotch bonnet pepper are cooked in the soup. Cassava wafers used to be served with pepperpot soup but the light wafers seem to have been blown away by hurricane Gilbert. Now pita bread or, as the Jamaicans say, Syrian bread, cut in wedges and toasted, is served with the gumbo-like favourite.(p. 148)

1½ lb.	*callaloo*
½ lb.	*kale*
12	*ochroes*
½ lb.	*yellow yam*
½ lb.	*coco*
4 qt.	*water or stock*
½ cup	*coconut milk (optional) (p. 148)*
¼ lb.	*salted beef*
½ lb.	*pickled pig's tail*
½ lb.	*stewing steak, cut up*
¼ lb.	*shrimps*
1	*green pepper*
1	*clove garlic*
2	*stalks escallion*
	flour and salt for dumplings (p.149)

1 Cut salted beef and pig's tail in 1 inch cubes and soak in cold water to get rid of excess salt. (They can be soaked overnight if meat is very salty.) Strain.

2 Put beef and pig's tail in 4 qt. of water with cut up meat (not shrimps) to cook. This will take 25-30 minutes in the pressure cooker, or about 2 hours in a large saucepan.

3 In the meantime, wash callaloo and kale well, and when the meat is cooked, add the callaloo.

4 When callaloo is cooked (about 10-15 minutes), take out of stock and puree in a blender or food processor.

5 Cut up ochroes. Peel yam and coco and cut in 1 inch cubes.

6 Add ochroes, yam, coco, green pepper and garlic to stock.

7 Make spinners.(p. 149)

8 Add dumplings, and return callaloo and kale to pot. Simmer for 45 minutes approximately or until soup is thickened.

9 About 15 minutes before serving, add escallion, thyme and coconut milk, (claimed to be the secret of delicious pepperpot.)

10 Add shrimps and cook for about 5 minutes more.

11 Serve hot with pita bread.

Serves 8-10

Easy Green Peas Soup

This soup can be made in a jiffy using the blender. An excellent soup with very little fuss.

1½	*cups chicken stock*
1	*10 oz. can of peas*
½	*of a medium size onion*
1 tbsp.	*flour*
2 tsp.	*butter*
1 tsp.	*sugar*

1 Put all ingredients in blender and blend until smooth.

2 Heat mixture just until flour is cooked. Serve hot.

Serves 4

Red Peas Soup

Red peas soup is usually made as a one pot meal. Yam and sweet potato as well as spinners are cooked in the soup, which is usually served on wash day since it takes little attention.

1 pt.	*kidney peas*
4 qt.	*water*
1½ lb.	*soup meat (or stewing beef)*
¾ lb.	*pig's tail or ham (optional)*
1	*whole unbroken green scotch bonnet hot pepper (or any other green, hot pepper)*
1	*sprig fresh thyme or ⅛ teaspoon dried thyme*
½ lb.	*potato or yellow yam or coco*
3	*stalks escallion*
	salt
	spinners (optional) (p. 149)

1 Soak pig's tail overnight to remove excess salt. You may also soak red peas overnight.

2 Place soup meat, pig's tail and/or ham, cut in pieces, with peas in a large soup kettle or pot with about 4 quarts of water. Bring to the boil and then simmer for approximately 2 hours until peas are cooked.

3 Add seasoning, cut up potatoes, yam or coco and whole unbroken hot pepper.

4 Cook soup for about 30-45 minutes more and when soup is cooked, remove pepper and discard; for a smoother soup you may pass peas through a colander or sieve and rub with wooden spoon. Return to liquid and discard the pea skins, (Jamaicans like it with the peas whole.)

5 Taste for flavour and add salt to taste.

6 Add more boiling water if necessary. This soup should be moderately thick.

7 Serve with croutons.

Serves 6.

Green Gungo Peas Soup

1 lb.	*shelled green gungo or pigeon peas*
1 lb.	*stewing steak*
½	*pickled pig's tail or other salted beef, ham or ham bone*
2 qt.	*water*
1 lb.	*yellow yam*
½ lb.	*sweet potatoes*
	dumplings
	escallion
	green pepper
	thyme

1 Cut up and soak salted meat to remove excess salt.

2 Put all meats in water. Bring to the boil, add gungo peas and boil until almost cooked.

3 Add yam, potatoes, dumplings, thyme, escallion and green pepper.

4 Simmer uncovereduntil soup is thickened about 30 minutes.

Serves 6

Lobster Bisque

1 pt.	*lobster broth*
1 tbsp.	*flour*
2 tbsp.	*butter*
1 tsp.	*salt*
¼ tsp.	*pepper*
½ cup	*cooked lobster meat*

1 If using fresh lobster, boil shell and claws for about 30 minutes in 1 pt. water and use broth. If using canned lobster, use milk.

2 Place all ingredients in the blender in order indicated and blend until contents are partially blended (about 15 seconds.)

3 Heat until hot but do not boil. Serve hot.

Yields about 2½ cups.

Red Peas Soup with Pita Bread

Mannish Water

Curried goat is very popular in Jamaica and a goat is usually slaughtered for a 'feed'. The head, legs, liver etc. are used to make a soup called Mannish Water. A stock is made from what is available, usually called the 'fifth quarter' (see p. 90) Green pepper, green bananas, yam, coco and dumplings are added. The soup is usually made in a large pot to ensure everyone can have seconds, if they so desire. White rum, which is often served at these feeds, may be tipped in to satisfy the individual taste. I have no doubt it may taste good in china soup bowls, but hot paper cups are the norm for serving this brew. So much is left to the cook's discretion, that with two different cooks you may never capture the same taste.

4 lb.	*goat's head, tripe and feet (get butcher to cut in small pieces.)*
12	*green bananas*
1 lb.	*flour for spinners (p. 149)*
3-4	*hot peppers*
1 lb.	*coco*
½ lb.	*carrots*
½ lb.	*turnips*
3	*chochos*
3	*gallons water*
½ lb.	*escallion*
4	*sprigs thyme*
2 lb.	*yam*
	salt to taste

1 Chop meat into small pieces (if not already chopped.)

2 Wash and place in a 5 gallon container with 3 gallons of hot water.

3 When the water returns to the boil, simmer until meat is cooked soft (about 2½-3 hours).

4 Peel green bananas and add all other ingredients, except for flour, i.e. vegetables, seasonings etc. Cook uncovered for one hour more.

4 Use flour to make spinners (p. 149). Add to stock.

5 Correct seasoning and remove hot peppers. Add more water if necessary.

6 Serve hot.

Serves - the village!

Cook's Tip

Many people find that a spoonful of the gravy from the curry goat greatly improves the Mannish Water while others prefer to add some rum to the brew.

Summer Soup

Here is a cold soup you may relish on a hot summer's day or evening.

2 cups	*water*
1 lb.	*ripe tomatoes*
½	*medium cucumber*
¼	*medium onion*
4 oz.	*sherry*
1 tsp.	*sugar*
½ tsp.	*salt*
4 tbsp.	*cream*
	pinch of pepper

1 Wash vegetables and blend in 2 cups of water.

2 Strain and extract juice.

3 Blend juice with other ingredients except the cream.

4 Chill in the refrigerator.

5 Prior to serving stir in cream.

Serves 4

Spicy Pumpkin Soup
(with Ginger)

2 lb.	*soup bones or stewing steak*
½ lb.	*pickled pork (optional)*
2	*stalks escallion*
1	*sprig thyme*
2 lb.	*pumpkin*
1	*clove garlic*
1 lb.	*yam*
1	*whole green pepper*
	about ½ in. Jamaican ginger root, minced
4 qt.	*water*

1 Place soup meat and pork in about 4 qt. cold water to boil until meat is cooked.

2 Add yam, pumpkin and other seasoning (except gingers). Boil until pumpkin and yam are soft. Remove pumpkin, blend or crush pumpkin and return to stock. Take out whole pepper and discard.

3 Taste and correct seasoning, if necessary.

4 Add ⅛ tsp. minced ginger to each soup plate.

5 Serve hot.

Serve 6

Cook's Tip

Soup meat and pork can be cooked in the pressure cooker in about 30 minutes to shorten cooking time.

Cream Of Pumpkin Soup

2 tbsp.	*butter or margarine*
3 tbsp.	*flour*
2 cups	*milk*
1	*onion, chopped*
2 cups	*boiled pureed pumpkin (1 lb.)*
1 tsp.	*granulated sugar*
	salt and black pepper to taste

1 Melt butter and fry onion.

2 Add flour, salt, pepper and sugar and cook well.

3 Add milk slowly, stirring so butter and flour are well blended with milk.

4 Stir until smooth and thickened.

5 Combine pumpkin with mixture.

6 Simmer for 5 minutes. Serve hot.

Serves 4

Cream of Pumpkin Soup

Cold Cream of Avocado Soup

1	*medium avocado (pear)*
1 cup	*chicken stock*
2 cups	*whole milk*
½	*an onion*
1 tsp.	*sugar*
1 tsp.	*Pickapeppa sauce (available in speciality stores)*
	salt (optional)

1 Peel and chop avocado and onion.

2 Put all ingredients in blender and blend. Add more milk if too thick and salt, if necessary.

3 Chill and serve with a slice of avocado on top.

Serves 6

Cream Of Callaloo Soup

2 tbsp.	*butter*
2 tbsp.	*flour*
2 cups	*milk*
1	*onion, chopped*
½ lb.	*callaloo*
	salt and black pepper to taste

1 Wash and boil callaloo (reserve water).

2 Put callaloo in blender container with about 1 cup of water from boiled callaloo and process on high until smooth.

3 Heat saucepan. Add butter and saute onion.

4 Add flour and make a blonde roux. (See white sauce p. 97)

5 Pour cold milk on hot roux and stir with wooden spoon until flour is cooked and milk thickened.

6 Add salt, pepper and callaloo puree. Stir and simmer 5-10 minutes.

7 Serve with boiled shrimps or crisp bacon on top.

Serves 3-4

Cucumber Soup

½ oz.	*butter*
4	*pimento grains*
½ pt.	*milk*
1	*onion*
2	*medium cucumbers*
1 pt.	*chicken stock*
1 tsp.	*salt*
1 tsp.	*sugar*
	parsley and lime to garnish

1 Chop onion finely and fry gently in butter.

2 Add chopped cucumber (do not remove all skin.) Fry for 1 minute.

3 Add chicken stock, cover saucepan, and simmer gently for 15 minutes.

4 Remove from heat, cool and sieve or use electric blender to puree. Add pimento, salt and sugar.

5. Stir in milk and chill.

6 When cool, put in freezer, remove ½ hour before serving to ensure there are no lumps of ice. Garnish with chopped parsley and lime.

Serves 5-6.

Cold Iced Rum Soup

1	*10 oz. can beef consomme*
2 tbsp.	*dark Jamaica rum*
	escallion
	lime
	crushed ice

1 Stir the rum into the comsomme and chill overnight.

2 To serve, sprinkle with chopped green escallion tops. Serve with a thin slice of lime on a bed of crushed ice.

Serves 3

TO MARKET, TO MARKET

Mention vegetables and most Jamaicans think of the vegetables they cook in their one pot soup. Ital (no salt) foods which the Rastafarians cook - also the ever-growing army of vegetarians are changing the green taste of Jamaica. Callaloo, which we use to make our pepperpot soup and team with seafood to make our Florentine dishes, flourishes everywhere. Barbers plant it between haircuts, some have even switched and all they now cut is callaloo, or greens as they prefer to call it.

We are full of beans. The world may know it as kidney beans but we call it red peas; susumber we rename gully beans and pigeon peas we call gungo peas. The fact is we use any lentil in combination with whatever is available, but the trio of trotters, tripe and oxtail is definitely married to broad beans.

Although we do have unusual and interesting vegetables, we are still in the process of learning to use them innovatively.

Rice and Peas

Rice and peas is usually rice and red kidney beans, Jamaica's 'Coat of Arms' in cooking. (Dried gungo peas, or green, when in season, are also used.) The proportions vary from household to household, but a ¼ pt. of dried peas or a ½ pt. of freshly picked red peas or gungo to 1 lb. rice is adequate. Dried peas are put on in cold water, green peas are put on in boiling water.

¼ pt.	*dried red peas*
1 lb.	*rice*
½ pt.	*green gungo peas*
2	*stalks escallion*
	thyme
2 tsp.	*salt*
1 tbsp.	*sugar*
1	*dry coconut*
	milk from 1 dry coconut

1 If dried peas are used, wash well before soaking and boil in the same water until cooked enough, but **not too much** water should be used as coconut milk is also to be added. (If dried peas are used soak for 2 hours, if peas are freshly picked (green) no soaking is necessary.).

2 When peas are nearly cooked, add rich milk from very dry coconut (p. 148), bringing liquid to about twice or 2½ times the quantity of rice to be used. See that pea grains are not broken.

3 When peas are cooked, add seasoning. Wash rice and add to peas. When water boils again, reduce heat and cook on slow fire. Rice should be tender and all the liquid absorbed. (Near the end of cooking time, if the grains are not quite cooked, and it is not advisable to add more water - place a piece of Saran wrap instead of foil on top of rice and cover. This usually finishes the cooking satisfactorily.)

4 When cooked, stir with a fork before serving.

Serves 6

Cook's Tip

If preferred use margarine or butter and cow's milk, powdered skim milk or evaporated milk instead of coconut milk. If desired, fry a few strips of bacon, cut into small pieces and add.

Crunch Slaw
(A Type of Cole Slaw)

1 lb.	*cabbage*
¼ lb.	*carrots*
4 oz.	*raisins, washed and dried*
4 oz.	*nuts (almonds or walnuts are fine)*
	mayonnaise

1 Shred cabbage.

2 Grate carrots on the coarse side of the grater.

3 Mix in nuts and raisins with enough mayonnaise to moisten.

4 Chill and serve on a bed of lettuce.

Serves 6

Bean Salad

1 cup	*cooked red kidney peas*
1 cup	*cooked broad beans*
1 cup	*cook string beans or any combination of cooked or canned beans you like*
1 cup	*sweet pickle*
1	*onion, juiced*
¼ tsp.	*white pepper*
5	*hard-boiled eggs, sliced*
¾ cup	*diced celery*
1 cup	*mayonnaise*
1	*green pepper, sliced.*

1 Mix all ingredients together and serve chilled.

Serves 6

Bean Salad

Doved Peas

Green gungo peas are usually harvested in December. Higglers spend their time between serving customers, shelling the gungo or pigeon peas, as they are called. Jamaicans on the whole, use much of them green, in soups, stews, with rice, and in rice and peas, so much so, that precious little survives to see the sun and get dried. Lucille Jackman serves this dish with flair, from her adopted Barbados. Once I had some repairs done to my house and Mrs. Sylvia Hendricks arranged a party, at which she cooked the Jamaican version of Doved Peas. She mixed the cooked gungo peas with creole saltfish, topped by crisp, fried corn pork and served with roasted, yellow heart breadfruit. Everyone was impressed with how delicious this simple mixture could be.

It is difficult to state quantities because it is such a favourite whenever cooked, but allow at least:

6 cups	*green gungo peas*
1 tsp.	*salt*
1	*large onion, minced*
1	*red sweet pepper, cut up*
1	*green sweet pepper, cut up*
2 tbsp.	*butter*
	bacon cuttings and bits of ham (optional)

1 Boil 6 cups green gungo in enough water to cover.

2 Add 1 teaspoon salt (if you have bacon cuttings available and bits of ham, use some in the water boiling the peas.)

3 Put the remainder of the bacon and ham with some minced onion, and red and green pepper in a frying pan and fry in butter until cooked.

4 Add the cooked gungo and stir mixture in frying pan until cooked.

5 Remove from heat and stir in a little butter.

Serves 6-8

Mushroom Croquettes

This recipe for croquettes with a real Jamaican twist, came from the Scientific Research Council.

2 cups	*finely mashed, cooked breadfruit or cooked potato*
1 lb.	*fresh oyster mushrooms, washed,dried and chopped*
1 oz.	*butter or margarine*
1	*onion, finely chopped*
1	*egg*
	salt and pepper to taste
	oil for deep frying

1 Saute mushrooms and onions in butter, then remove from flame.

2 Beat egg lightly.

3 Combine mashed breadfruit or potato with mushrooms, onions and seasoning.

4 Add enough of the egg to make for easy handling of mixture.

5 Flour hands and roll into balls.

6 Fry in hot oil until just golden brown.

Yields 24

Cook's Tip

To cook breadfruit - peel and remove centre from mature breadfruit. Cut in slices and boil in salted water. When properly cooked breadfruit should be soft but not falling apart.

Crunch Slaw

Fried Ochroes

½ lb.	*ochroes*
¼ cup	*cornmeal*
¼ cup	*flour*
1	*egg*
	pinch of salt
¼ cup	*oil*

1 Wash ochroes and drain.

2 Mix cornmeal, flour and salt set aside.

3 Separate egg yolk from white. Beat egg yolk then add white.

4 Drop whole ochroes in egg then in cornmeal mixture to coat.

5 Heat oil in heavy skillet and fry ochroes until lightly browned on all sides being careful not to puncture them.

6 Put ochroes on paper towel to drain.

7 Sprinkle with salt and serve hot.

Serves 4

Sweet Potato in Orange Skins

4	*medium sized sweet potatoes*
¼ tsp.	*grated nutmeg*
2	*eggs*
½ cup	*sugar*
½ tsp.	*orange rind*
1 tsp.	*salt*
2 tbsp.	*margarine*
1 tsp.	*cinnamon*
1 cup	*orange juice*
6	*oranges*

1 Make orange cups by cutting oranges into halves and taking out pulp, leaving skin intact.

2 Boil potatoes with ¼ cup sugar, 1 tsp. salt and enough water to cover.

3 Mash potatoes while still warm and add nutmeg, orange rind, margarine, cinnamon and eggs.

4 Add enough orange juice to make mixture of piping consistency.

5 Using a rose tip in a piping bag, pipe potato mixture into orange skins.

6 Bake for 20-30 minutes at 350° F until potato is cooked through.

7 Serve hot.

Serves 6

Sweet Potato in Orange Skins

Quiche Without Pastry

2	*medium onions, sliced*
1	*can evaporated milk*
3	*large eggs (4 if medium sized)*
2 tbsp.	*margarine*
	garlic powder
	salt and pepper
½ cup	*grated cheddar cheese*
	parmesan cheese (optional)

1 Preheat oven to 350° F.

2 Saute onion slices in margarine or oil until transparent (not brown.)

3 Beat eggs until light.

4 Add can of evaporated milk and seasoning to eggs.

5 Spread onion slices in bottom of a pie plate.

6 Pour milk and egg mixture over onion slices, and sprinkle grated cheese on top, if desired.

7 Parmesan cheese and/or paprika can be sprinkled on top.

8 Bake for 30-45 minutes.

9 Serve with mustard sauce. (p. 96)

Serves 4-6

Cook's Tip

Marshmallows may be put on top after removing from oven.

Stuffed Pumpkin

1	*4 lb. pumpkin with stem*
1 cup	*chopped onions*
2 tbsp.	*oil*
2 lb.	*fish fillet*
1	*medium green pepper chopped*
¼ tsp.	*black pepper*
¼	*scotch bonnet pepper (optional)*
1 cup	*tomatoes*
2	*eggs beaten*
	bread crumbs

1 Wash pumpkin, slice the top off the pumpkin where the stem is and remove seeds and membrane.

2 Plunge whole pumpkin in boiling, salted water for 10-15 minutes.

3 Remove and drain.

4 Cube fish.

5 Sauté seasoning in 2 tbsp. oil.

6 Scoop out flesh from pumpkin and add to seasoning.

7 Add eggs and fish to the mixture. Stuff pumpkin with the mixture. Sprinkle top with breadcrumbs, and bake for 1 hour at 350° F.

8 Slice pumpkin in pegs and serve.

Serves 6-8

Stuffed Pumpkin

Baked Stuffed Chochos

8 oz.	*minced beef*
½ tsp.	*salt*
½ tsp.	*black pepper*
1 tsp.	*sugar*
1	*clove garlic*
1	*stalk escallion*
1	*sprig thyme*
1	*large onion, finely chopped*
3	*large chochos*
1 tbsp.	*margarine*
¾ cup	*bread crumbs*
½ cup	*grated cheese*

1 Put thawed mince in saucepan, with enough cold water to cover.

2 Beat mince with fork, so that there are no lumps.

3 Add onion, garlic, escallion and thyme.

4 Simmer until meat is almost cooked. Add salt and correct seasoning.

5 Cut chochos in halves and boil in salted water until almost cooked about 25 minutes.

6 Scrape out the insides with a spoon. Leave the half shell intact to be filled with meat. Set aside.

7 Crush the flesh of the chocho and mix with the cooked mince. Add pepper, salt and sugar. Cover and simmer for a few minutes to finish cooking chocho and blend the flavours.

8 Carefully fill half shells with mixture, sprinkle with bread crumbs, dot with margarine or butter and bake in 350° F. oven until crumbs are brown.

9 Sprinkle with cheese, as soon as it comes out of the oven, so cheese is just melted, but not cooked hard. Serve hot.

Serves 6

Bammy

The art of making bammies is dying out, because many feel it can only be made in the parish of St. Elizabeth by the experts. If you see bitter cassava in the market, why not buy 2 lb. and try your hand at making some?

2 lb.	*bitter cassava or*
1½ lb.	*grated cassava*
Pinch of salt	

1 Peel and grate the cassava.

2 Place in a clean muslin cloth.

3 Wring out and discard the juice.

4 Add salt to the cassava 'bran'.

5 Place about a cup of the mixture in a small, greased, heavy and shallow frying pan. (The size of the frying pan will determine the size of the bammy.)

6 Press down with the bottom of a bottle or similar implement.

7 Place the pan over a moderate heat. In a few minutes as the pan heats up, some steam will rise.

8 When the edges shrink slightly from the sides of the pan, flatten the mixture and turn it over to cook the other side.

9 The process should take approximately 10 minutes for each side.

10 Repeat the process until all the cassava is used up. The bammies can be refrigerated for up to 14 days or frozen.

11 When ready to use the bammies, soak them in milk, water or coconut milk for about 5-10 minutes.

12 Either fry or grill until light brown. They can be buttered before placing on grill or immediately they are taken off and served hot. Serve with fried fish or saltfish and ackee.

Yields 4

Fried Ochroes (right)
Baked Stuffed Chochos (left)

Golden Bammy Slices

2	*six inch bammies*
3 cups	*cold water*
½ tsp.	*salt*
1 oz.	*soft margarine*

1 Cut each bammy in 4 pieces.

2 Soak in water for 5 minutes. (Slices should be completely submerged.) Check bammy, it should not be too soft, as some bammies have very little starch to hold them together. Soak longer if bammy is still hard.

3 Pour off water and spread with margarine.

4 Grill about 8 minutes on one side and 5 minutes on the other.

5 Steam in a steamer until cooked.

6 Fry in deep fat until golden brown or fry in fat about ½ inch deep.

Serves 4

Potato Cheese Casserole

1 cup	*milk*
3	*eggs*
1 tsp.	*salt*
½ tsp.	*pepper (optional)*
1 cup	*cubed cheddar cheese*
1	*green pepper, cut up*
1	*onion, quartered*
4	*medium potatoes (1¼ lb.), pared and cubed*

1 Preheat oven to 350° F.

2 Grease ovenproof casserole dish.

3 Put all ingredients in blender in order listed. Cover and run on liquefy. (Do not over blend.)

4 Pour in casserole and bake for 1 hour.

5 Serve hot.

Serves 4

Vegetable Casserole

2 lb.	*vegetables e.g. carrots, chochos, string beans, parboiled potatoes etc.*
1	*large onion, sliced*
1 tsp.	*salt*
3 tsp.	*butter or margarine*
3 tsp.	*flour*
2 cups	*milk*

1 Preheat oven to 350° F.

2 Grease a medium casserole dish with butter.

3 Peel and slice vegetables.

4 Layer half of vegetables in casserole dish with sliced onions.

5 Mix flour and salt.

6 Sprinkle half of flour mixture on sliced vegetables and dot with half of butter.

7 Layer remaining sliced vegetables and sprinkle with remainder of flour mixture. Dot with remaining butter.

8 Pour milk over and bake for 45 minutes to allow sauce to cook.

9 Serve hot.

Serves 4-6

Vegetable Casserole

Pepper

Easy Potato Casserole

4	*medium potatoes*
1	*large onion, sliced*
½ tsp.	*salt*
1 tbsp.	*flour*
1 tbsp.	*butter*
1 cup	*milk*

1 Preheat oven to 350° F.

2 Peel and thinly slice potatoes.

3 Put ½ of the potatoes into a greased, ovenproof dish.

4 Sprinkle with ½ salt and ½ flour.

5 Add ½ onions and dot with ½ butter.

6 Pour ½ cup of milk over the potatoes.

7 Cover with remaining potatoes, salt, flour, butter and onions. Add balance of milk.

8 Bake at 350° F for 1¼ hours or until potatoes are cooked.

Serves 4

Corn Fritters

1 lb.	*can whole kernel corn*
1½ cups	*sifted all purpose flour*
2 tsp.	*baking powder*
¼ tsp.	*salt*
2 tbsp.	*sugar*
2	*eggs beaten*
	milk
	oil for deep frying

1 Drain can of corn and save liquid.

2 Make up liquid from the can to 1 cup with milk. Set aside.

3 Sift together flour, baking powder, salt and sugar.

4 Combine beaten egg, milk mixture and corn.

5 Add to dry ingredients and mix just until flour is moistened.

6 Drop batter by tbsp. into deep, hot oil (375° F.)

7 Fry until golden brown, (about 3 minutes.)

8 Drain on paper towel.

9 Serve with warm Maple syrup.

Yields 18

Corn Pudding

3 eggs	*lightly beaten*
2 cups	*drained and cooked or canned whole kernel corn*
2 cups	*milk, scalded*
½ cup	*finely chopped onion*
1 tbsp.	*butter, melted*
¼ cup	*sugar*
1 tsp.	*salt*

1 Combine ingredients and pour into greased 1½ qt. casserole.

2 Set in shallow pan with boiling water.

3 Bake at 350° F for 40-45 minutes. or until knife inserted in centre comes out clean.

4 Let stand 10 minutes. (Centre will firm up.)

Serves 6

Vegetable Lasagna

White Sauce:

⅓ cup	*margarine or butter*
⅓ cup	*all purpose flour*
1 tsp.	*salt (optional)*
⅛ tsp.	*ground nutmeg*
3 cups	*milk*

Filling:

1 lb.	*callaloo*
2 cups	*Ricotta cheese (or Cheddar)*
½ cup	*grated Parmesan cheese*
1 tsp.	*dried basil crushed (or 2 tsp. fresh basil, chopped fine)*
1 tsp.	*dried oregano*
½ tsp.	*garlic powder*
½ tsp.	*pepper*
12	*lasagna noodles, cooked and drained*
1½ cups	*shredded Mozzarella cheese*
8 oz.	*fresh mushrooms, sliced and sauteed in butter*
2	*medium carrots, sliced*
1	*medium onion, chopped*
1	*medium green pepper, chopped*

1 Grease 13 x 9 baking dish.

2 Steam callaloo, cool and set aside.

3 Melt margarine in 1 qt. saucepan, over low heat.

4 Stir in flour, salt and nutmeg.

5 Cook over low heat, stirring constantly until bubbly.

6 Remove from heat. Stir in milk.

7 Heat to boiling, stirring constantly. Boil for 1 minute.

8 Cover and keep warm (if sauce thickens, stir in a little milk.) Set aside.

9 Mix callaloo, Ricotta cheese, Mozzarella cheese, ¼ cup Parmesan cheese, basil, oregano, garlic powder and pepper.

10 Arrange a layer of lasagna, cheese mixture, and vegetables (mushrooms, carrots, onions and green pepper) in the greased baking dish and pour over ½ of the white sauce. Repeat steps but finish with a layer of lasagna. Top with slices of Mozzarella cheese. Finish off with a sprinkling of nutmeg or paprika. Top with slices of Mozzarella cheese. Finish off with a sprinkling of nutmeg or paprika.

11 Cook lasagna uncovered in 350° F. oven until bubbly (about 35 minutes.) and top is golden brown.

12 Let stand 10 minutes. before serving.

Serves 8

Cook's Tip

Always cover white sauce to prevent skin forming.

CATCH OF THE DAY

Fish in Jamaica is fish at its very best. There is no part of Jamaica which the day's catch cannot reach in excellent condition.

A great deal of fish is sold on roadsides and in markets where vendors will scale and gut the fish when it is bought. Jamaican housewives wash fish in plenty of lime juice, dry and season it, usually with garlic, salt and pepper.

The head of the fish is eaten and enjoyed in Jamaica or used to make fish tea. Jamaicans have a saying 'if you 'fraid for eyes you can't eat head'. We suspect it's not the eyes of the fish to which they are referring, since most Jamaicans eat fish head with the eyes in place and usually use this saying when someone is staring at them.

Guide To Jamaica's Best Loved Fish

Salted Fish (Codfish)

Salted fish (or Saltfish as we say in Jamaica) is a very useful item in our diet, because it can be kept without refrigeration. Jamaicans hardly think of saltfish as seafood, perhaps because cod is not caught in the Caribbean and fresh cod is hardly available here. Salted cod is a native necessity to accompany ackee and for fritters and codfish balls, since a small piece goes a long way. It goes well with callaloo, as a *ceviche* raw with vinegar, onions and pepper served on crackers and is heaven-sent as an accompaniment for pear and hard dough bread. Ask any Jamaican rum drinker about 'pick up' saltfish.

King Fish

This is usually bought in ½ to 1 inch slices and preferred by those who do not like to deal with fish bones.

Sprats

These are usually fried very crisp and most of the bones eaten. Again scotch bonnet pepper, vinegar and onions are the accompaniments for this small fish, washed down with lemonade or the popular Jamaican Rum.

Snapper

For most Jamaicans, snapper is the first fish which comes to mind when asked the name of a fish. Butter fish, Parrot and other tropical fish are also available in 1 lb. size and are eaten fried, steamed, escoveitched, baked, roasted or jerked. The black marks on the snapper are supposed to be the fingerprints of Jesus, as it is said this was the fish used in the feeding of the five thousand.

Blue Marlin

This is a welcome addition to our Jamaican menu, rolled with capers and presented in a cold plate, or as an appetizer.

The annual October Blue Marlin Tournament in Port Antonio attracts many fishermen who may share their catch, preserve them, or eat what they can and smoke what they can't.

Pickled Mackerel

Pickled Mackerel, like codfish, is not thought of as sea food. It is used to make the famous Mackerel 'Rundown' (see p. 67), or used with boiled green bananas in a dish called 'Dip and Fall Back' (see p. 67).

Pickled Shad

Not as popular as Mackerel because of the bones, it is still, however, a favourite of many. It is usually cooked with its garnish as a package in quailed, green banana leaves, tied with the bark of the banana and boiled, a parcel you can post any day to the well known Jamaican photographer, Amador Packer.

Conch (or Sea Snails)

Not as popular in Jamaica as in the Turks and Caicos Islands, where Conch fritters are fast food, and the Bahamas which boasts a delicious Conch Salad and Conch soup. The meat is very tough and has to be tenderized, usually by pounding, but the flavour is worth the trouble.

Lobster

If you are a lover of lobster, try not to visit Jamaica in the closed season, although wise hotel food and beverage managers usually have stocks in store to tide them over that lean period. The small, red, spotted lobsters, called chicken lobsters, are popular in Jamaica. Larger ones, fresh from the sea, are halved, grilled, curried or served in a salad. Grilled lobster is usually the favourite because, like a good wine, 'it needs no bush'. The dried shells of lobsters are hung in warehouses storing flour to keep out weevils.

Crab

Crabs are delicious just boiled with pepper, salt and green bananas, usually in a big pot or the meat can be picked and stuffed in the back as crab back.

Shrimp

Shrimp is more readily available than lobster. It is usually served butterfly in batter, in Chinese food, curried, in Callaloo soup (see page **30**), stir fried or in a creole sauce. Pepper shrimp is sold at Middle Quarters by the bridge in the parish of St. Elizabeth. Shrimp are sold fresh or frozen, imported with or without the head, cooked, deveined and graded into 120 to the lb., down to 15 or less to the lb. The Chinese buy them dried for rice dishes.

Baked Fish

Fillet and cutlets or large cuts of fish seem to lend themselves better to baking.

1 lb.	*fish*
1 tbsp.	*lemon juice*
1	*egg, beaten*
2 tbsp.	*milk*
2 tbsp.	*dried bread crumbs*
1 tbsp.	*butter*
	salt and black pepper to taste

1 Prepare fish (see instructions for preparing fish on p. 150) and sprinkle with lemon juice, salt and pepper. Place in greased, ovenproof dish.

2 Pour 2 tbsp. of milk in the dish.

3 Brush fish with beaten egg and sprinkle with bread crumbs and dot with butter.

4 Bake for 15 to 20 minutes for small pieces of fish, or allow 10 minutes to each lb., and 10 minutes more for a large cutlet at 350° F.

Serves 2

Cook's Tip

Slices of tomatoes and bacon can be baked atop the fish. Serve with a suitable sauce. Any liquid in baking dish should be added to the sauce.

Escoveitched Fish with Bammies (front)
Batter Fried Fish and Festival (back)

Baked Stuffed Fish

For baking use large or medium sized fish, allowing 1 fish per serving, or use fish fillets or fish slices.

2 lb.	*fish*
1 cup	*flour*
1	*egg, beaten*
2 tbsp.	*bread crumbs*

Allow about 2 tbsp. of stuffing for each lb. of fish. You may use steamed callaloo, veal stuffing or forcemeat (bread crumbs, fresh herbs, margarine, lime juice, pepper and salt) or tomatoes, bread crumbs, ham and seasoning, to stuff the cavity.

1 Prepare fish for cooking. (See instructions on p. 150)

Large Fish:

Cut open the back of the fish and remove the bone, and fill with stuffing.

Medium Fish:

Fill the cavity with stuffing and sew up the opening, truss with a long skewer in the shape of an 'S'.

Fish Slices:

Remove the centre bone and fill the cavity with stuffing.

Fish Fillet:

Spread with stuffing and roll up from head to tail. Skewer or tie.

2 Dip fish in seasoned flour.

3 Coat with egg and bread crumbs or batter (See recipe for Batter Fried Fish)

4 Place in buttered baking dish, and bake in moderate oven 350° F about 20 minutes, basting occasionally.

5 Serve on a hot dish.

6 Remove skewer and thread if used.

7 Garnish with lime or lemon and parsley.

Serves 6

Escoveitched Fish

Escoveitched fish is very popular in Jamaica, and is eaten from morning until night, all over the island. Nearly any fish that swims in our waters can be subjected to this treatment. The fish is cooked and pickled in a tasty sauce of vinegar and spices and garnished with onion, chocho, carrots etc. Small whole fish, sliced fish, or sprat can be served for breakfast, lunch, dinner or as hors d'ouevres.

2 lb. *fish*
¼ cup *flour*
oil for frying

Escoveitch Sauce:

1 cup *vinegar*
1 cup *water*
pinch of salt
1 tsp. *sugar*
1 cup *julienne strips of chochos and carrots*
2-3 *medium size onions, cut into onion rings*
hot pepper to taste
6 *pimento grains*

1. Prepare fish for frying (see p. 150)
2. Lightly dust with flour
3. Fry fish in ½ inch deep oil.
4. As soon as flesh is opaque, fish is ready. Set aside.
5. Boil 1 part of water with 1 part of vinegar with a pinch of salt and a teaspoon of sugar.
6. Add julienne strips of chocho, carrots, hot pepper to taste, some pimento grains and onion rings.
7. As soon as liquid boils, pour over fried fish. This is done the day before it is eaten, and it is not kept in the refrigerator.

Serves 4-6

Cook's Tip

It is a good idea to fry fish in oil about ½ inch deep, as deep fat fries so quickly. (There is a tendency to over fry the fish and dry it out.) As soon as the flesh is opaque, it is ready to be eaten. Just a light dusting of flour should be used when frying fish that is going to be escoveitched.

Brown Stew Fish

Once I was interviewing a young man who came for a job as a cook. I asked him to give me an idea of what he would serve at a cocktail party, and without hesitation, he replied 'Brown Stew Fish'. Since on his application form he stated that his reading preference was 'friction' and 'non-friction', I felt satisfied to say 'NEXT'!

Jamaicans like Brown Stew 'anything', because they are very fond of gravy. It doesn't matter what kind of fish or how much of it they are cooking. The gravy can be from a bright tomato red to a pale blonde colour.

6 *slices of fish,*
or
6 *small fish*
2 *onions*
2 *tomatoes*
2 *stalks escallion*
any other vegetable in season
fish stock or water

1. Prepare and fry fish.
2. Strain nearly all the oil from frying pan, and set aside.
3. Sauté onions, tomatoes, escallion and other vegetables, in frying pan.
4. Add stock or water and simmer until flavours blend.
5. Add fish to sauce.
6. Cover and simmer until heated through.

Serves 6

Batter Fried Fish

2 lb.	*fish fillet*
1 cup	*flour*
2 tsp.	*baking powder*
1 tsp.	*salt*
1	*egg, separated*
½ cup	*lukewarm water*
1 tbsp.	*margarine*
	oil for deep frying

1 Prepare fillets for frying (see p. 150) Set aside.

2 Sift flour, baking powder and salt in bowl.

3 Drop egg yolk in centre.

4 Add water and margarine and mix well.

5 Fold in beaten egg white.

6 Dip seasoned fish fillets in batter.

7 Heat oil in frying pan and deep fry fish.

8 Drain on absorbent paper and serve hot with wedges of lime and sprigs of parsley, parboiled carrots, and slices of pepper.

Serves 4-6

Steamed Fish

2 lb.	*fish (can be sliced or whole)*
2 oz.	*butter or oil*
3	*medium onions, cut up*
2	*tomatoes*
2	*stalks escallion*
	sprig of thyme
1	*whole green scotch bonnet pepper with stem*
½ lb.	*carrots*
½ lb.	*chocho*
2 cups	*fish stock or water*

1 Clean and prepare fish (see p. 150)

2 Sauté onions in butter or oil. Remove and set aside.

3 Put escallion, thyme and all other vegetables in oil and stir fry.

4 Add stock or water and allow vegetables to cook.

5 When mixture is ready, add fish and onions. Take out whole green pepper and set aside. Simmer mixture of vegetables, fish and onions, without lid, for 15 minutes or until cooked.

Serves 6

Grilled Lobster

Grilled Lobster

Lobsters in Jamaica do not have large claws; they are really supposed to be large crayfish. We are not overly concerned, however, if they are lobsters or crayfish. What's in a name? They are absolutely delicious, and I promise you will never forget your first taste.

6 lb.	*lobster*
12 oz.	*butter (2 oz. for each lb. of lobster)*
6	*cloves garlic*
	lemon wedges
	salt and pepper to taste

1 Prepare lobster (see p. 150).

2 Season lightly with salt and pepper.

3 Brush generously with melted butter.

4 Turn on broiler on medium heat.

5 Place halves of lobsters, meat side up, on broiler rack.

6 Broil for 3-4 mins. or until lobsters are heated.

7 Heat remander of butter with cloves of garlic.

8 Brush garlic butter lavishly over lobsters. Garnish with lemon wedges.

Serves 6

Lobster Newburgh

In order to obtain lobster meat for this recipe follow steps for preparing lobster (p. 150)

3 cups	*lobster meat cut into large cubes*
1/4 cup	*butter or margarine*
2 tbsp.	*flour*
1/2 tsp.	*prepared mustard*
1 tbsp.	*minced onion*
1 tsp.	*salt*
1 1/2 cups	*light cream*
2 tbsp.	*sherry*
1 oz.	*grated cheese*

1 Melt butter and stir in flour, mustard, minced onion and salt.

2 Saute and slowly stir in cream. Cook until thickened.

3 Add lobster meat and sherry to mixture, heat.

4 Fill lobster shells and place in 1 1/2 quart casserole dish - sprinkle with cheese.

5 Brown under the broiler.

6 Garnish with lemon wedges and French fried onion rings.

Serves 3-4

Curried Shrimp

2 lb.	*fresh shrimp, cleaned and deveined*
2 tbsp.	*butter*
2 tsp.	*lemon juice*
2 tbsp.	*curry powder*
2	*onions*
3	*cloves garlic, minced*
3 tbsp.	*oil*
1	*small scotch bonnet pepper, cut up*
	salt and pepper to taste
2	*stalks escallion*

1. Saute chopped onions, escallion and minced garlic in oil.. Add curry.
2. After approximately 2 minutes, add shrimp, salt and pepper and a small piece of scotch bonnet (be cautious - scotch bonnet peppers are extremely hot). Cook shrimp for no more than 5 minutes (do not over cook). Mix well.
3. Mix in lemon juice and butter. Shrimp should be firm but tender.
4. Serve hot with white rice and a tossed salad.

Serves 4 - 6

Shrimp Pudding

1 lb.	*fresh shrimp, cleaned*
2 tsp.	*butter*
2 tbsp.	*oil*
3	*eggs beaten*
1 cup	*mashed potato*
1 cup	*milk*
1 tsp.	*salt*
3 tbsp.	*grated Parmesan cheese*
2 tbsp.	*cornstarch*
	bread crumbs

1 Saute shrimp in butter and oil until brown.

2 Combine beaten eggs, mashed potato, salt, cheese, cornstarch and milk, and mix in the shrimp.

3 Turn into buttered casserole, which has been dredged with bread crumbs.

4 Bake in 350° F. oven for 25 minutes until puffed and brown.

Serves 4

Shrimp Florentine

This delicious dish makes a quick vegetable and shrimp meal in a hot casserole and is a favourite of Noel and his wife Beverly Dexter, of singing fame.

7 cups	*callaloo, washed and cut up*
1	*onion, chopped*
4	*stalks escallion, cut fine*
1 tsp.	*salt*
1 tsp.	*black pepper*
1 lb.	*shrimps, cleaned and deveined.*

1 Put all ingredients, except shrimps, in a saucepan to cook. (No water is necessary to cook callaloo.)

2 Simmer for 10 minutes.

3 Make a medium white sauce. (See p. 97.)

4 Add callaloo to white sauce.

5 Mix in shrimps and bake at 350° F. for 15 minutes, just until shrimps are cooked and heated through.

6 Serve hot.

Serves 6

Shrimp Florentine (Following page Left)
Ackee and Saltfish with Pear (Following page Right) (front)
Johnny Cakes (back)

Ackee and Saltfish

Recently since the price of salted cod has sky-rocketed, there has been some juggling of the proportion of ackee to saltfish in Jamaica's national dish. In fact, ackee can now even stand alone with the usual accompaniments of onion, tomato and escallion. Ackee has also entered into some new marriages with mackerel, salted fresh fish, sardines, lobster, shrimps, cheese, curry, bacon and even pickled chicken. Jamaica is the only island in the Caribbean where ackees are eaten. Mavis Wilson, who worked as a nurse at a hospital in St. Thomas in the Virgin Islands, said there was an ackee tree on the hospital grounds but no one even touched the tree, not to mention the ackees, for which she was indeed grateful.

1 lb.	*saltfish (codfish)*
24	*ackees (or 2 tins canned ackees)*
1	*large onion, chopped*
	salt and pepper to taste
3	*cooking tomatoes diced*
1	*stalk escallion chopped*
1 tbsp.	*oil*

1 Soak codfish overnight. (It will not be necessary to cook it and it will not be trashy, as is the case sometimes, when it is boiled.) Remove skin when soaking, as a lot of the salt is in the skin or alternatively soak for 30-40 minutes, place in fresh cold water, bring to a boil, drain and repeat. Flake fish and set aside.

2 Fry some bacon strips or corned pork, and set aside.

3 Prepare ackees for cooking by removing seeds and pink lining. Boil for 20 minutes in boiling, salted water. Drain. (If using canned ackees just drain and stir into sauté mixture.)

4 Sauté onions, tomatoes and escallion. Add seasoning, bacon and ackees and sauté for approximately 5 minutes.

5 Add flaked saltfish to mixture, sauté briefly for flavours to blend.

6 Serve hot with Johnny cakes or boiled green bananas.

Serves 6

Cook's Tip

Remember to be sure that ackees have opened naturally. Be careful not to break up ackees when mixing for the serving dish. One way of serving without breaking up the ackees, is to put a border of ackees on a platter and fill the centre with codfish. Garnish with bacon, onion and sweet pepper rings.

Curried Crab and Rice

The first time I experienced Harold Edingborough's cooking was at a party called a 'Kussi ma'. This is Eddie's recipe as he gave it to me.

3	*crabs*
2	*limes*
1 tbsp.	*curry powder*
	pepper to taste
4 cups	*coconut milk*
1 lb.	*rice*
	salt and pepper to taste

1 Wash crabs with limes thoroughly and drain. Break open claws and pick out meat. Remove backs from crabs reserving any meat but discarding gill and intestine.

2 Season crab meat with salt, pepper and curry powder and leave to marinate for about 1 hour.

3 Place crab meat and rice in coconut milk and cook on a slow heat for ½ an hour. Let steam until properly cooked.

Serves 6

Mackerel Rundown
or
'Dip and Fall Back'

Buy pickled mackerel which is firm to the touch.

Allow 1 medium size, very dry coconut for each lb. of fish.

2 lb.	*salted mackerel*
3 pt.	*coconut milk*
1	*large onion, finely chopped*
1 tsp.	*vinegar*
1	*tomato, chopped (or 1/4 cup ketchup)*
1	*scotch bonnet pepper*
	lime juce

1 Having selected firm, fairly large mackerel, remove heads and wash in plenty of cold water. Use lime or lemon to help clean and flavour fish.

2 Soak in hot water for 2-3 hours, changing once or twice to remove surplus salt. Fish, however, must not be too fresh or it will be unpalatable.

3 When fish is about half soaked, prepare coconut milk in the usual method (see p . 148), extracting rich milk, about 1½ pints. for each lb. of fish.

4 Boil milk in a thick-bottomed dutch oven, or in a pressure cooker. This is the same process used for making coconut oil, but the sauce is used just before the milk turns to oil, when a sweetish custard is formed. A tsp. of vinegar, chopped onions, tomatoes and scotch bonnet pepper can be added to the custard. Flake the flesh of the mackerel and add to liquid, or if liked, the mackerel can be cut in pieces and added with the bones. Dumplings made of flour, or flour and grated, green bananas can be cooked in the gravy.

5 Serve with all the gravy and garnish with green sweet pepper.

Serves 6

Cook's Tip

Boiled green banana or roasted breadfruit is the ideal accompaniment for this dish and is a popular dish for brunch. Saltfish may be cooked in this way too. Shad may also be used, but this is a softer and bonier fish and requires careful handling.

Val Harrison's Mackerel

A friend of mine, Val Harrison cooks his mackerel in this unique way.

1 lb.	*mackerel*
1 tsp.	*lime juice*
12	*green bananas*
2-3 tbsp.	*cooking oil*
2	*onions, sliced*
1	*tomato*
2	*stalks escallion, chopped*
	scotch bonnet pepper to taste
	lime juice

1. Soak the mackerel overnight in plenty of warm water with lime juice.

2 The following day, put on enough water without salt to boil, to accommodate the bananas and mackerel.

3 Put in peeled green bananas. When almost cooked, about 30 minutes, carefully lay mackerel on top of bananas so that they keep their shape when cooked.

4 Place mackerel in serving dish.

5 In a large frying pan, sauté sliced onions, tomato, escallion and pepper in oil.

6 Pour over mackerel in serving dish and serve with boiled bananas.

Serves 4

THE HOT POT

Mention Jamaica to any foreigner and he immediately thinks of reggae music, Bob Marley and jerk cooking. This hot and spicy barbecue style of cooking has been with us for hundreds of years but in recent times has been transformed, from a type of cooking peculiar to one small area of Jamaica, to the streets, homes and restaurants of the world. There was a time when jerking was confined to pork; today buyers can enjoy jerk pork, chicken, fish and even jerk lobster from jerk 'pits' all over the island. The word pit comes from the traditional method of cooking; a charcoal fire is made in a shallow pit in the ground and small planks of green aromatic pimento wood are placed above the hot coals to form a crude grill. The highly seasoned meat is stretched across this wooden grill in large slabs (in the case of chicken, the whole chicken), covered with a top layer of wood and left to cook slowly. The 'real' jerk taste comes from a combination of the blend (and quantity) of the seasoning used, the effect of the smoke created by the twin layers of green aromatic wood and the slow method of cooking.

At Boston Bay in Portland, on the north-east coast of Jamaica, there is a cluster of jerk pits and the potential purchaser is allowed to move from pit to pit sampling tiny morsels from each one, before deciding which is the best of the lot.

This is outdoor cooking at its best. Now it is possible not only to enjoy the genuine article on the spot from the traditional cooks but to prepare home-style jerk by purchasing the jerk seasoning right there at the jerk pit.

Mackerel Rundown

Jerk Chicken

3	*whole chickens cut in halves*
6	*cloves of garlic, finely chopped*

Jerk marinade:

2 tsp.	*ground Jamaican pimento*
½ tsp.	*grated nutmeg*
½ tsp.	*mace*
1 tsp.	*salt*
1 tsp.	*sugar*
2 tsp.	*thyme*
1 tsp.	*black pepper*
1½ cups	*escallion*
2	*onions*
2	*scotch bonnet peppers*
2 tbsp.	*cooking oil*

1 Cut 3 chickens in halves. Rinse chicken in lime water, drain and season with the garlic.

2 Blend all the ingredients for the marinade together in a blender or food processor. (To grind pimento, heat grains in a frying pan in a tablespoon of oil until crisp and then blend.)

3 Pour mixture on to seasoned chicken and leave to marinate for about 2 hours or overnight.

4 Light barbecue grill, make sure coals are white before putting on meat. Put on chicken halves skin side down, and keep turning to prevent the chicken from getting too dark. Allow to cook slowly.

5 Chop into small pieces. Can be served with additional jerk sauce.

Serves 12

Cook's Tip

It is the combination of the seasonings that gives the jerk its unique flavour.

Fricasseed Chicken

This is the most popular way of cooking chicken in Jamaica. It is really braising chicken, with as many additions as there are cooks, and since fricasseed chicken is usually eaten with rice and peas, the rich tasty gravy is well appreciated. Most Jamaican men like gravy and lots of it, possibly because we eat most of our meats with rice and not potatoes. They feel that good gravy is just as important as love in a good marriage. As a matter of fact, whatever they like, they like it in quantity.

1	*whole chicken*
3 tsp.	*salt*
1 tsp.	*sugar*
½ tsp.	*black pepper*
3	*cloves garlic*
2	*stalks escallion*
	sprig of thyme
2 tbsp.	*oil*
2 cups	*water or chicken stock*
1 tbsp.	*Pickapeppa sauce*
1½ tbsp.	*tomato ketchup*
½ lb.	*potatoes*
¼ lb.	*carrots*
1	*medium chocho*
2	*large onions*

1 Prepare chicken. Cut up, wash, drain and season chicken. (See p. 149.)

2 Heat oil and add chicken. Brown just enough to stiffen chicken.

3 Add water or stock, with Pickapeppa and tomato ketchup.

4 Rough chop vegetables, add to chicken and simmer for 15 minutes, stirring occasionally.

5 Serve hot in gravy.

Serves 4-6

Cook's Tip

Chicken is a white meat and gravy should not be too dark.

Barbecued Chicken

Our warm climate, allows us to have barbecue all year round. At times the barbecue, even at home, is not successful because enough time is not allowed for the coals to be ready, before putting on the chicken. Always allow at least 2 to 2½ hours for the chicken to be properly done on the grill (1 hour of that time is for the burning of the coal, for the coal to be perfectly white before putting on the chicken.) It is a good idea to do a few extra chickens when you light the barbecue grill, as the taste the next day may be better.

4 *whole chickens*

Wet Seasoning:

8 *cloves garlic*
6 *stalks escallion*
1 *sprig fresh thyme or 1 tsp. dried thyme*
1 tbsp. *vinegar*

Dry Seasoning:

6 tbsp. *salt*
2 tsp. *sugar*
1 tsp. *black pepper*

Barbecue Sauce:

2 cups *vinegar*
2 tbsp. *granulated sugar*
1 tsp. *salt*
1 tsp. *dry mustard*
1 tsp. *paprika*
1 tsp. *black pepper*
2 tbsp. *oil or margarine*
1/2 cup *tomato ketchup*

1 Mix all ingredients of barbecue sauce together in a saucepan. Simmer for 15 minutes and then cool. Set aside.

2 Cut chickens in quarters, rinse in lime water (do not squeeze lime on chicken in water) and drain before adding seasoning.

3 Blend garlic, escallion and thyme in the blender with 1 tsp. vinegar. (It is better not to mix the seasonings together.) Put on the wet seasoning (garlic etc.) before putting on the dry seasoning.

4 Rub in dry seasoning and leave for at least 2 hours (overnight is better.)

5 Pour barbecue sauce over chicken and leave to marinate for at least 2 hours.

6 When ready to barbecue, light the coals. Burn until coal appears white (no coal should have a flame.) Put chicken on grill. The chicken should have enough space between the coal and the chicken.

7 Grill skin side down, turning frequently with a pair of tongs to prevent burning. Do not pierce chicken.

9 Put cooked chicken aside, on the grill, so it keeps hot and completes the cooking process.

Yields 16

Cook's Tip

If the coals are white when the chicken is put on the grill, it is better to put the barbecue sauce on the chicken **before** it is put on the grill.

Fricasseed Chicken with Rice and Peas (Following page Left)
Barbecued Chicken (Following page Right)

Oven-Baked Chicken

Even if this dish has to be prepared well in advance of being served, it will not become tough as will fried chicken. It can be served hot or cold and it takes less oil to cook.

1	*3-4 lb. chicken cut up or chicken parts*
2-4	*cloves of garlic*
2	*stalks escallion*
1	*sprig of fresh thyme (¼ teaspoon dried thyme)*
1 tbsp.	*vinegar*
3 tsp.	*salt*
1 tsp.	*sugar*
½ tsp.	*pepper and any herb or poultry seasoning you may like with chicken*
½ cup	*white breadcrumbs*

Sauce:

½ cup	*evaporated milk*
½ cup	*tomato ketchup*
2 tbsp.	*melted margarine*

1 Preheat oven to 350° F.

2 Mix sauce ingredients and leave to blend.

3 Rinse chicken in lime water and drain.

4 Cut up garlic, escallion and thyme very fine and blend in blender with 1 tbsp. vinegar. Season chicken with these ingredients and leave to soak for 10 minutes

5 Season chicken with dry ingredients (salt, sugar, pepper and any other poultry seasoning.)

6 Add sauce to chicken and marinate for at least 30 minutes.

7 Put chicken in greased, shallow baking tin, sprinkle on dry, but not brown bread crumbs.

8 Bake for 1 hour exactly, no longer. (In fact, if the oven is hot, look at it in 40-45 minutes.)

Serves 4

Chicken Salad in Pineapple Shells

2	*small pineapples cut in halves lengthwise*
1½ cups	*cooked chicken (in cubes)*
½ cup	*raisins*
½ cup	*coconut*
½ cup	*yoghurt*
¼ cup	*mayonnaise*

1 Cut pineapple flesh away from shells and set shells aside.

2 Cut chicken flesh into cubes.

3 Place pineapple flesh in bowl with chicken, coconut and raisins.

4 Combine yoghurt and mayonnaise

5 Add to chicken and pineapple. Toss.

6 Pile back into prepared shells, and serve chilled.

Serves 4

Chicken Tikka

Barbara Abramson, from the United Nations Women's club in Jamaica, demonstrated this chicken dish on a local television show I did in 1985. Called Chicken Tikka, it is from the Punjab region of India.

2-3 lb.	*chicken pieces (leg and thigh)*
	chili powder
	fresh limes
	salt (if desired)
	equal parts of butter and oil

1 Preheat grill or broiler of stove.

2 Remove all skin from chicken. Score each piece deeply in waffle (criss-cross) design.

3 Apply chili powder over chicken parts liberally. Salt lightly (or not at all.)

4 Leave for ½ an hour, for powder to be absorbed.

5 Squeeze lime juice over each piece.

6 Place under grill, but not too close, and baste with mixture of equal parts butter and oil.

7 Grill until golden brown, turning pieces as necessary. Total cooking time is about 20-25 minutes.

8 Arrange on platter and garnish attractively. Serve with hot rice and tikka sauce.

Serves 4

Tikka Sauce

natural yoghurt
fresh mint
garlic (optional)

1 Mince fresh mint very fine.

2 Mix with yoghurt.

3 Minced fresh garlic may be added if desire.

Chicken Roll

1	*3½-4 lb.chicken*
2	*stalks escallion*
3	*cloves garlic*
	sprig of thyme
	black pepper and salt to season chicken

Stuffing:

4	*slices of bread (grated or blended)*
1	*onion chopped fine*
2 tbsp.	*margarine*
1 tsp.	*salt*
½ tsp.	*black pepper or to taste*
2	*eggs*

1 Debone chicken and season (see p. 149) Leave for at least half an hour to marinate.

2 Preheat oven to 350° F.

3 If using a stuffing, hard boil 2 eggs by putting in cold water to simmer for 20 minutes. Cool by adding cold water, crack shell all around and strip.

4 Saute cut up onion in margarine.

5 Add bread crumbs and seasoning. Cook and cool.

6 Spread open seasoned chicken and shape into a square.

7 Put cooled stuffing on chicken allowing a border ½ inch without stuffing.

8 Place eggs with narrow ends touching in centre of stuffing.

9 Roll lengthwise carefully into a roll and secure with skewers, tie in shape with cord.

10 Making sure to keep roll in shape lightly brush with cooking oil before putting on rack in baking tray, cut side down.

11 Bake no longer than 1¼ hours at 350° F.

Yields 20 slices

Chicken Roll (Following page Left)
Chicken Salad in Pineapple Shells (Following page Right)

Jamaican Curried Chicken

Usually served with steamed rice and green bananas. There are many ways of making curried chicken. The main ingredient, curry powder, is a subtle blend of spices which greatly determines the taste of the finished dish. It is a good idea to experiment with different blends of curry powder.

1	*whole chicken 3-4 lbs.*
2	*limes*
3	*cloves garlic*
2	*stalks escallion*
¼ inch	*root ginger*
1½ tbsp.	*curry powder*
	a pinch of pimento
1 tsp.	*sugar*
2 tsp.	*salt*
2 tbsp.	*oil*
2 cups	*water*
3	*medium potatoes*

1 While frozen, cut chicken in 1½ to 2 inch serving pieces. (If cut when frozen, the bones will not splinter and will be better enjoyed at eating time.)

2 Juice limes in water; quickly wash chicken in the water and drain.

3 Blend garlic, escallion, and ginger, leave for 30 minutes.

4 Mix curry powder and a pinch of pimento with sugar and salt. Rub on chicken. Leave for a further hour.

5 Brown chicken in 2 tbsp. oil. Keep turning until curry powder is cooked. Add 2 cups of water and 3 medium potatoes cut in cubes. As soon as liquid starts boiling, turn down the heat and allow to simmer until chicken is cooked, approximately 20-30 minutes. chicken should be tender.

6 Dress up curry chicken with accompaniments and serve with flair. The usual accompaniment is Mango Chutney, but slices of dried coconut without the dark skin, pineapple chunks, orange segments, ripe bananas, raisins, grated carrot, cucumber slices and yoghurt, can be served.

Serves 6

Cook's Tip

It is necessary to cook the curry seasoning well, but be careful not to overcook the chicken.

Orange and Ginger Chicken

(from the kitchen of Candis Stona)

Having cooked chicken on national T.V. for over a year without repeating a recipe, I am always on the lookout for recipes that are uncomplicated and interesting to the housewife. In a matter of minutes Candis Stona, Busha Browne's charming wife, wrote out this easy and delicious recipe for me.

1	*chicken in serving parts*
	salt and pepper to taste
3	*cloves garlic, crushed*
1	*medium onion chopped*
¾ cup	*of orange juice (ortanique juice is Candis' preference)*
2 tbsp.	*honey*
½ in.	*root ginger*
2 tbsp.	*soy sauce*
3 tbsp.	*sugar*
½	*sweet pepper (green pepper)*

1 Cut up and season chicken with salt, pepper, garlic and onion.(p. 149)

2 Combine remaining ingredients in a bowl and mix well.

3 Pour sauce over chicken in a shallow baking dish.

4 Bake at 375° F. for one hour, basting regularly.

5 Serve with rice and green salad.

Serves 4-6

Pot Roast of Chicken

My brother Martin thinks this is the best chicken dish, so much so that he learnt to cook it.

1	*3-4 lb. whole chicken*
1	*sprig thyme*
2	*cloves garlic*
2 tsp.	*salt*
1 tsp.	*sugar*
6	*stalks escallion*
1	*medium onion, rough chopped*
2 tbsp.	*cooking oil*
2 tbsp.	*oyster sauce*
2 tbsp.	*soy sauce*

1 Rinse chicken in lime water and drain well. Do not cut up. Take off wing tips.

2 Season with thyme, garlic, salt and sugar. Marinate for 1 hour.

3 Beat (or bruise) escallion and rough chop.

4 Stuff cavity of chicken loosely with escallion and chopped onion.

5 Heat dutch oven or heavy saucepan with lid for 1 minute.

6 Add 2 tbsp. of cooking oil.

7 Brown chicken on one side for about 15 minutes. leaving the lid on.

8 Turn. Allow 10 minutes. for the other side, still keeping the lid on. Leave covered for a further 5 minutes.

9 Leave to simmer on low heat for a further 15-20 minutes or until cooked. Test with a fork.

10 When chicken is cooked remove escallion and onion from cavity and blend with soy sauce and oyster sauce. Set aside.

11 Cut chicken into serving pieces. Pour sauce over warm chicken.

12 Heat and serve in sauce.

Serves 4-6

Chicken Pelau

Since this is a one pot meal that traps the flavour of the ingredients, you will soon find for yourself how difficult it is to spoil the dish. The Hylton sisters, Phyllis and Isolyn, cook a really tasty Pelau and I think their recipe originated in Panama. Dr. Margaret Green demonstrated a Trinidad version, at a Consumer's League Fair. The caramel was a secret given to her by her mother.

1	*3 lb. chicken or chicken parts*
2	*stalks escallion*
2	*cloves garlic*
	Pinch of ground pimento
2 tbsp.	*oil*
2 tbsp.	*granulated sugar*
2 cups	*raw rice*
1	*onion*
4 cups	*chicken stock or water*
1 cup	*coconut milk*
2 tsp.	*salt*
2 tbsp.	*margarine*
2	*young carrots (optional)*
1	*green pepper (optional)*
1 cup	*cooked peas (optional)*
1	*can niblet corn (optional)*
	any leftover vegetables

1 Wash chicken in lime water. Drain and season with escallion, garlic and pimento. Leave to marinate for ½ an hour.

2 Heat oil in dutch oven or skillet and add sugar. Allow to caramelize to add colour to the dish. (Granulated sugar caramelizes better than brown sugar.)

3 Add chicken and cook just enough to allow chicken to stiffen and obtain a rich, brown colour.

4 Add rice and chopped onion. Sauté about 5 minutes.

5 Add stock, coconut milk and all other ingredients. Cook until rice is ready.

6 Serve hot.

Serves 6

Oven Baked Chicken (Following page Left)
Ham Croquettes (Following page Right)

Canard A L'Orange

(Duck in Orange Sauce)

Most people think of duck as a Chinese dish. This dish was cooked by Mrs. J. McNeil as the French contribution in a series of cooking demonstrations of 'Christmas around the world' - very easy and quite tasty.

1	*7 lb.duck*
2 tsp.	*salt*
1 tsp.	*sugar*
½ tsp.	*of freshly ground black pepper*
2 oz.	*vegetable oil*
4	*carrots, sliced*
4	*onions sliced*
5 oz.	*white wine*
1 pt.	*white stock or water*
	juice and rind of 1 orange
2	*oranges, peeled and quartered.*
1 tsp.	*cornstarch or arrowroot*
	Pinch of sugar

1 Rinse and dry duck thoroughly. Season duck with salt, sugar and black pepper.

2 In a skillet, heat vegetable oil. On very moderate heat, brown duck lightly. Pour off oil.

3 Add carrots and onions, pour wine over all and increase heat. Cook without covering the pot, until there is only about 3 tbsp. of liquid left.

3 Add stock or water. Correct seasoning.

4 Cover and put to simmer for approximately 1 hour or until tender.

5 Peel orange with vegetable peeler, being careful to get only the zest.

6 Shred zest. Put in small saucepan with just enough water to cover and boil for 5 minutes Strain well.

7 Peel 2 oranges as for salad, and quarter for decoration.

8 Strain the liquid from the duck and skim off fat. Approximately 8 oz. of liquid should remain. If more, reduce, if less add water or stock to make 8 oz.

10 Thicken with cornstarch or arrowroot.

11 Add juice of 1 orange, pinch of sugar and the orange rind. Remove from fire.

12 Serve by slicing duck into serving pieces.

Serves 3

Oxtail

2lbs	*oxtail*
2	*onions minced*
½ cup	*escallion cut up*
½pt	*broad beans (dried) or 1 tin*
	thyme to taste (about 1 teaspoon dried or 2 teaspoons fresh)
1½ tsp	*salt*
2	*tablespoon cooking oil*
2	*cloves garlic*

1 Season oxtail and allow to marinate for at least 1 hour in a covered container in the refrigerator.

2 Use a heavy saucepan (or pressure cooker), heat oil and brown well. Pour off oil and add water a little at a time; also add broad beans.

3 Cover and cook on a low simmer until meat and beans are very tender. (If using pressure cooker put enough water to cover meat and beans and pressure for 30 mins. or until tender).

4 Carrots, spinners (long dumplings) onions or any vegetable of your choice may be added to gravy. (Do not pressure the vegetables.)

Serve with enough gravy to cover meat.

Serves 4

To Cure A Ham

Pork is undergoing a change of image as well as nutritional profile and is now called 'the other white meat'. It is said that pork produced today has 50% less fat than that of only 20 years ago while remaining nutritious. Pork is a rich source of protein, thiamine and niacin, while it is low in sodium, calories and cholesterol. It is fat, however, that keeps meat tender, so cook very lean pork with care. Pork cooked to an internal temperature of 160° F for medium 'doneness' will provide tender juicy flavourful results.

Pork used to be overcooked for fear of trichinosis, but trichinosis is said to be destroyed at 137° F. and is clinically rare today.

You will not need a meat pump, as you will be processing the leg when it is frozen. You need not buy expensive pickling salt, but the rule of good cooking is never more applicable than when making a ham; start with good ingredients.

10 lb.	*of frozen pork (select a back leg)*
½ lb.	*salt*
1 tsp.	*powdered mace*
1 tsp.	*grated nutmeg*
4 oz.	*brown sugar*
2 tsp.	*salt petre*
	pickling spice

1 Select a back leg weighing not less than 10 lb. from a well fed pig. Any and every leg of pork just won't do! It is well to have the leg well frozen at least 3 days, but a week is best.

2 Mix the above ingredients thoroughly (salt, mace, nutmeg, sugar, salt petre and pickling spice) and divide the mixture in two parts.

3 Rub ½ of the mixture on the frozen leg, until all of it is absorbed. (Put away remaining ½ of mixture to use another day.)

4 Put leg in heavy plastic bag with cut side down, so that it will absorb pickle that falls to the bottom of the bag.

5 Place in refrigerator.

6 After 7 days rub in remaining salt mixture. (This time the leg must not be frozen.) Return to plastic bag as before.

7 Allow 2 days for each 1 lb. of meat for curing. So it will take approximately 3 weeks to cure a 10 lb. leg.

8 When leg is cured, package for freezer until ready for use.

To Cook A Ham

Glaze:

½ cup	*of brown sugar*
1 tsp.	*of prepared mustard*
3	*dozen whole cloves*

Wash off salt, and treat as mild cured ham. The lower the heat, the softer the ham will be.

1 Cook at 325° F for approximately 3 hours.

2 Trim off skin, and glaze by mixing sugar and mustard together.

3 Brush mixture over ham.

4 Score the surface in ¾ inch squares or diamonds.

5 Stick whole cloves in middle of squares. If you wish you may dress with pineapple, orange slices or cherries.

6 Bake 30 minutes longer. (A meat thermometer will remove all the guesswork - just watch the mercury rise to tender ham.)

Serves 40-60

Cook's Tip

Cut the skin in squares, brush with oil and return to oven until crisp. Serve as hors d'oeuvres or a tasty snack.

Ham Croquettes

An easy yet delicious way of using left-over ham.

3 tbsp.	*butter or margarine*
⅓ cup	*sifted flour (for sauce)*
1 cup	*milk*
2 cups	*coarsely ground, or finely chopped ham*
1 tbsp.	*finely chopped onion*
1 tsp.	*prepared mustard*
1	*beaten egg*
½ cup	*fine cracker crumbs*
½ cup	*of flour (for dip)*
	oil for deep frying

1 Melt butter and blend in flour.

2 Add milk and cook over low heat, stirring constantly, until thick.

3 Cool. Add ham, onion and mustard and chill.

4 Shape either in balls, pyramids, or barrels.

5 Dip in the flour, then in the beaten egg, then in crumbs. Let stand a few minutes.

6 Fry in deep fat at 375° F. for 7 to 8 minutes or until brown.

7 Drain on paper towels.

Yields 12

Oven Pork Chops

2 lb.	*pork chops*
4	*cloves garlic*
1 tsp.	*salt*
1 cup	*brown sugar*
1 tsp.	*prepared mustard*
2 cups	*cider*

1 Season pork chops with garlic and salt.

2 Mix sugar and mustard and spread mixture on both sides of chops.

3 Place in a ovenproof dish (ovenproof dish should not be greased) and pour cider over chops.

4 Bake at 350° F. until done.

Serves 4-5

Pork Chaw Sow

5 lb.	*pork rib*
1/4 tin	*(about 2 oz. drained weight) red bean curd*
1 tbsp.	*black bean (wash trash off black beans)*
5	*cloves garlic*
1 tsp.	*5 spice powder*
6 tsp.	*star aniseed*
2 tbsp.	*rum*

1 Wash and dry pork.

2 Rub all seasonings on pork and let soak overnight.

3 Open flat and score.

4 Roast in preheated oven at 350° F. for about 2 hours.

Serves 8

Chinese Pork & Yam

For this dish you will need an enamel basin, about 10 inches in diameter and a larger pot, or steamer, to set the basin in.

4 lb.	*chinese spare ribs*
4 lb.	*yellow yam*
½ tin	*red bean curd (4 oz.)*
1 tsp.	*5 spice powder*
1 tsp.	*star aniseed*
4 tsp.	*salt*
1 tsp.	*sugar*
4	*cloves of garlic chopped fine*
1 tbsp.	*browning or honey*
2 tbsp.	*oil*
4 oz.	*white rum*
	salt (to rub on yam)

1 Season spare ribs with red bean curd, 5 spice powder, star aniseed, salt and sugar. Rub on garlic and browning or honey. Leave to marinate, preferably overnight.

2 Pour 2 tbsp. oil in frying pan or dutch oven.

3 When oil is hot, place spare ribs in oil, skin side down. Brown and turn over. Cook just enough to allow pork to get stiff.

4 Cut ribs into serving pieces, pour over white rum and let it soak in.

5 Peel yellow yam and cut in serving pieces.

6 Sprinkle salt on yam, rub over surface, and leave 5-6 minutes. This will get rid of the slime that is usually on the cut yam.

7 Wash off yam and pack side by side with pork, skin side down in basin.

8 Rest basin on a rack in steamer and steam about 3 hours.

Serves 12

Pot Roast of Beef

Many Jamaicans believe that certain dishes have to be cooked in certain pots. They swear tripe and beans do not taste as good when cooked in a pressure cooker, as when cooked in an iron pot, on a coal pot stove. The same is true for stew peas and oxtail, as well as potato pudding. Even though the modern hustle does not allow time for cooking these dishes in the iron pot, on the coal stove, Pot Roast of Beef is found in many iron dutch pots atop modern stoves and cookers. Mention of roast beef and the dark gravy-rich pot roast causes many to salivate and dream about the rest of the menu; usually rice and peas, fried plantain, a salad, and a scotch bonnet pepper.

4-5 lb.	*cut of beef without bones*
4 tsp.	*salt*
1 tsp.	*pepper*
	a sprig of thyme
2	*stalks escallion*
2 oz.	*beef suet*
2 tbsp.	*oil*
	Water
	onion rings

1 Season overnight with gashes filled with salt, pepper, thyme, escallion and beef suet.

2 Tie to keep shape and it is ready for the pot.

3 Heat dutch oven with the lid on.

4 Pour in 2 tbsp. oil and heat before putting in the beef.

5 Brown on all sides, then cover and allow to simmer with about ½ cup of water. (You may need up to a quart of water, but continue adding only ½ cup at a time.) The secret of getting it soft and not trashy is to use low heat. If the meat is fully cooked, a fork should go into the meat easily.

6 When it is soft enough, season gravy, add onion rings, and heat until just cooked.

7 Cool meat and slice.

8 Serve with gravy on slices.

Serves 8-10

Jerk Pork

5 lb. *pork*

Seasoning:

1 *onion*
1 cup *escallion*
5 *cloves garlic*
2 tsp. *fresh thyme*
1 *scotch bonnet pepper without the seeds*

Jerk marinade:

5 tsp. *salt*
2 tsp. *sugar*
2 tsp. *ground pimento*
¼ tsp. *ground nutmeg*
¼ tsp. *ground mace*
1 tsp. *black pepper*

1 Rub in seasoning on pork. Leave for ½ an hour.

2 Rub on jerk marinade and leave to marinate for at least 5 hours (overnight is better.)

3 Prepare grill, and barbecue pork, until cooked, or put in hot oven 400° F. for about 20 minutes. Lower oven temperature to 275° F. and allow to cook slowly until done.

4 Chop into small pieces when ready to serve.

Serves 6

Cook's Tip

Allow a teaspoon of salt to a lb. of pork (use 5 teaspoons salt to 5 lbs of pork - a lot of salt is used, both for taste and as a preservative.). Remember 'the juice should run clear, but it should still be there.'

Spare Ribs

4 lb. *spare ribs*
2 tbsp. *rum*
2 tbsp. *sugar*
3 *large stalks of escallion, cut up*
2 tbsp. *all purpose soy sauce*
2 dsp. *oil*
½ inch *dried mangarine skin*
black pepper (optional)
1 cup *cornstarch*
salt
oil for frying

1 Soak mangarine skin in cold water.

2 Parboil spare ribs with a little salt for about 10 minutes. Cool and cut in ribs.

3 Scrape the white pulp from mangarine skin and cut finely or in fine shreds and mix with the rum, sugar, escallion, soy sauce, oil and black pepper.

4 Leave ribs to soak in marinade overnight.

5 Next morning sprinkle on cornstarch and rub in.

6 Fry ribs.

7 Put in a basin and cover with foil. Lift foil at both ends.

8 Put water in pressure cooker, rest basin on rack and pressure at 15 lb. for about 7-10 minutes.

Serves 6

Jerk Pork (Following page Left)
Pickled Cow Tongue (Following page Right)

Cow Foot

In the distant past when sugar was king, the roasting joint, the fillet and other prime cuts of beef went to the Great House. Workers who reared the cattle usually took for themselves the tail, the head, the tripe and the feet of the cow. What the workers got was called the 'fifth quarter'. The 'fifth quarter' cuts required long, slow cooking but even now workers' preference is for the fifth quarter. In Jamaica, most people cook cow foot but they make calves feet jelly, or cow heel stew. Our men think any gooey food like this is good for them. Cow foot is savoury and calves feet jelly is sweet. Some persons cook enough cow foot to use some in a stew and use the balance to make the jelly. In the days of the shutpans, I understand higglers used to treat calves feet jelly as a street food, and deliver it door to door chilled, lemon and strawberry being the two favourite flavours.

3 lb.	*cow foot*
3 qt.	*water*
	pinch of salt
2	*stalks escallion*
2	*cloves of garlic*
	sprig of thyme
	black pepper to taste
	vegetables of your choice

1 For the stew and jelly, cook 3 lb. cow foot chopped in 3 inch pieces.

2 Add to 3 qt. water, with a pinch of salt.

3 Boil or cook in pressure cooker approximately 40 minutes or until soft.

4 Remove cow foot from liquid, and place cow foot and 2 cups of the liquid in saucepan to make stew. Stew may be made with or without bones.

5 Set aside the remaining liquid to make jelly.

6 Skim fat from liquid (a few leaves of lettuce passed over the fat will help to get rid of it.)

7 Add seasonings and vegetables (carrots, chochos, potatoes) to stew. (Approximately 30 minutes.)

8 Serve hot.

Serves 4

Calves Feet Jelly

Sugar or condensed milk to taste

1 Sweeten reserved liquid from cow foot with sugar and flavouring to taste or use condensed milk to sweeten.

2 Pour into serving dishes and leave to set in the refrigerator.

Serves 6

Pickled Cow Tongue

There is a Jamaican proverb which says 'is no want of tongue mek cow no talk' and when you see the tongue of a cow you will agree. Despite not talking, most cow tongue can find itself in a pickle - try this tasty recipe.

1	*cow tongue*
7	*glasses cold water*
1 dsp.	*brown sugar (a little less than a tablespoon)*
1 tsp.	*salt petre (nitrate)*
3 tbsp.	*fine salt*

1 Mix all ingredients together to make a brine and boil for 2 hours.

2 Leave tongue in brine for 3 or 4 days, turning every day.

3 To cook, use ½ brine and ½ cold water and boil for 1½ hours.

4 Strip the tongue whilst hot.

5 To mould, roll tongue and put in basin with 2 tbsp. water in the bottom of the basin.

6 When set, slice and serve cold.

Yields 20 slices

Stew Peas

Red peas or kidney beans, whether stewed in soup, or cooked with rice and coconut milk, are the most used and best liked of the legumes. Some people cook the peas with a little baking soda, others use garlic pounded to help soften the grains, but the more popular way to soften dried beans is to soak in cold water. Salted meats are used to improve the flavour of the dish, and the bone from the Christmas ham makes its entrance in red peas or gungo soup.

1 pt.	*red peas*
½ - 1 lb.	*salted pig's tail,cut up*
½ lb.	*salt beef (pickled beef) or ham*
½ lb.	*beef stew, cut up*
1	*whole green scotch bonnet pepper*
2	*stalks escallion*
	sprig of thyme
2 cups	*coconut milk (optional)*
	salt and pepper to taste
	spinners (p. 149)

1 Soak peas in water to soften (overnight is best.)

2 Soak salted meat in lots of cold water, to get rid of the salt. (Again overnight is best.)

3 Place the meat and peas together in a large saucepan with enough water to cover (add the coconut milk here if desired). Simmer for about 2 hours or until soft.

4 Add thyme, escallion and the whole green scotch bonnet pepper. Make sure the stem is intact, if you only want the flavour. Add spinners.

5 Correct seasoning and cook until flavours are mixed for approximately 30 minutes. Serve hot with plain steamed rice, boiled sweet potatoes or fried ripe plantains and a slice of pear, a combination which will make any Jamaican salivate.

Serves 4-6

Stewed Tripe and Broad Beans

I usually call tripe the passion food. You either love it, or hate it with a passion. Jamaicans like the local tripe, but prefer a mix of local and imported.

1 lb.	*local tripe*
1 lb.	*imported tripe*
	juice of 1 lime
1 tbsp.	*cooking oil*
1 oz.	*margarine*
8 oz.	*uncooked broad beans*
2 tsp.	*salt*
	spinners
8 oz.	*potatoes, peeled and cubed*
2	*stalks escallion*
1	*sprig thyme*
2 tbsp.	*tomato ketchup*
1	*green scotch bonnet pepper with stem (for flavour)*
	other vegetables (optional)

1 Cut tripe in small pieces. Split and clean thoroughly.

2 Add lime juice to 1 qt. water. Rinse tripe thoroughly in lime water and drain.

4 Heat oil and margarine in frying pan, add tripe and lightly brown.

5 Place in pressure cooker and add enough water to generously cover tripe.

6 Add beans and salt.

7 Pressure for 20-30 minutes or until beans and tripe are soft.

8 Make spinners and add with all other ingredients, seasonings, vegetables etc. Simmer until done.

9 Correct seasonings and serve hot on heated plates.

Serves 5-6

Jamaican Curried Goat

In Jamaica we have more goat than sheep. Many Jamaicans do not think they are at a party, if curried goat is not served. It is the done thing to buy a goat and have it butchered for the occasion, in order to be able to use the head, feet and the offal to make 'Mannish Water' which takes pride of place at the party. Like the chicken, it is better to have the goat cut when partially frozen, to avoid splintering the bones. Allow time for the meat to thaw and drain, before seasoning. Always remember if the meat has water, it will dilute the seasoning. Some cooks brown the goat in oil before adding water, others cover the seasoned meat and allow it to steam in its own juices. Allow each lb. of goat to cook slowly for approximately 20 minutes. If the goat is cooked before serving time, turn off the heat and allow flavours to mix, then reheat before serving.

2 lb.	*mutton (goat)*
1	*stalk escallion*
2	*cloves garlic*
1 tsp.	*salt*
½	*hot pepper (optional)*
2 tbsp.	*curry powder*
1 tsp.	*salt*
2 tbsp.	*oil*
2 cups	*water*
1 lb.	*potatoes, peeled and cubed*

1 Season mutton with escallion, garlic, pepper, curry powder and salt and allow to marinate for at least 30 minutes (preferably overnight).

2 Scrape seasonings from meat and set aside before putting meat to fry in 2 tbsp. oil.

3 Brown meat. Add about 2 cups of water and simmer until soft.

4 Add more water if necessary.

5 Return seasonings and add potatoes to meat. Simmer until cooked about 2-3 hours.

6 Serve hot with the same accompaniments as curred chicken.

Serves 3-4 or 1 hungry Jamaican

Roast Suckling Pig

1	*12-15 lb.pig*
1 cup	*vinegar*
10	*cloves garlic*
4	*stalks escallion*
10 tsp.	*salt*
3 tsp.	*sugar*
3 tsp.	*black pepper or*
	2 scotch bonnet peppers, cut up
2	*sprigs thyme*
4	*medium onions, cut up*
2 cups	*breadcrumbs*
3 lb.	*yam or potatoes*
1 cup	*oil*

1 Rinse and dry pig. Wipe thoroughly, inside and outside, with vinegar. Leave to drain.

2 Saute onion and breadcrumbs.

3 Make stuffing by boiling yam until soft, crushing while hot and mixing with onions and bread crumbs. Set aside.

4 Season pig with garlic, escallion, salt, sugar, pepper and thyme. Place skewer in mouth of pig to keep it open.

5 Stuff the cavity of the pig loosely with the mixture.

6 Smear oil lightly over outside and score the skin.

7 Cover with foil especially the ears which may burn quickly.

8 Bake at 350° F. (35 minutes per lb.)

9 Pour off excess oil as it accumulates, to allow skin to become crisp.

10 30 minutes before end of calculated cooking time remove foil, replace skewer with an orange in the mouth and continue to cook for 30 minutes more, to ensure that meat is well cooked and brown. (Pork should always be well done.)

11 Allow to cool for 30 minutes before carving.

Serves 10 approx.

Curried Goat

DRESS IT UP!

Be careful how you mention sauce in Jamaica. To be 'served a sauce' is to teach you a lesson you may not care to learn.

Our savoury sauces are served in quantity but the sweet sauces are served with a heavy hand.

At Christmas, the pudding may be served with a choice of sauces, Hot Wine sauce, Hard sauce or many versions of Rum sauce being the most popular.

White sauce is used to serve creamed vegetables, macaroni and cheese and with lobster and shrimp.

Jamaicans love Mango Chutney with curried goat or curried anything and June Plum relish is now quite a favourite, while Avocado dip without the onion goes well with bullas.

Salad Dressing

Jamaicans use a lot of condensed milk because we like sugar and sweetened condensed milk does not spoil in the hot climate. Here is a recipe for a salad dressing using sweetened condensed milk.

1	*tin condensed milk*
1 tsp.	*salt*
1 cup	*vinegar*
2 tsp.	*dry mustard*

1 Beat all ingredients together in a bowl.

2 Leave a few minutes to thicken.

3 Refrigerate. Thin with vinegar or water as necessary.

Yields 2 cups

Sauce for Corned Beef

1 cup	*ketchup*
6 tbsp.	*red wine vinegar*
6 tbsp.	*honey*
6 tbsp.	*mint jelly*
3 tbsp.	*butter or margarine*
2 tbsp.	*prepared mustard*
1 tbsp.	*ginger*

1 Heat all ingredients to boiling, stirring constantly. Cool and bottle.

Yields 1½ cups

Mayonnaise

Mayonnaise is quite likely the most used sauce and it is very easily made in a blender.

2	*eggs*
1½ tsp.	*dry mustard*
1 tsp.	*salt*
1 tsp.	*sugar*
¼ tsp.	*paprika*
2 tbsp.	*lemon (or lime) juice*
2 tbsp.	*vinegar*
1¾ cups	*salad oil*

1 Put eggs, mustard, seasonings, lemon juice, vinegar, and ½ cup oil in blender.

2 Blend for 30 seconds on low.

3 Continue adding the remaining oil in a continuous stream through the opening in the blender cover until thick.

4 Refrigenate

Yields 3 cups

Cook's Tip

If you have added oil too quickly and sauce separates, pour it from the jar, put another egg in the blender jar and pour back the sauce that separated in a slow stream until it thickens.

Cottage Cheese Sour Cream

Use as a base for dips and on baked potatoes or salads.

½ cup	*milk*
1 tbsp.	*lemon/lime juice*
1 cup	*creamed cottage cheese*

1 Blend all ingredients together until smooth.

Yields 1½ cups

Mustard Sauce

Use on ham and corned beef or pickled tongue.

1 egg, lightly beaten
½ cup white sugar
¼ cup vinegar
1 tsp. dry mustard

1 Mix sugar and dry mustard.

2 Stir in beaten eggs.

3 Heat and stir until almost boiling.

4 Add vinegar by degrees and continue to stir until thickened. Cool and serve.

Serves 4

Avocado Dip

12 oz. cottage cheese
2 tbsp. lemon juice
1 small onion
1 avocado, diced
Dash of salt

Blend all together on medium speed. Chill and serve.

Yields 2 cups

Orange June Plum Relish

2 cups sliced June plum flesh
½ peeled orange, without seeds
¾ cup powdered sugar

1 In blender put orange and June plum.

2 Process on high until orange is partially grated.

3 Stop blender, add sugar and continue on low speed until well grated.

Yields 2½ cups

Substitute for Cream

¾ pt. milk
1 tsp. flour
yolk of 1 egg
½ tsp. sugar

1 Mix flour, egg and sugar.

2 Boil the milk and stir briskly in the flour mixture.

3 Pour back into saucepan and beat over the fire until it thickens but do not let it boil.

4 Use when cold.

Yields 1½ cups

Tartar Sauce

1 cup mayonnaise
2 tbsp. minced parsley
1-2 tbsp. minced dill pickles
1-2 tbsp. minced onion
1 tbsp. olives and/or capers (optional)

1 Stir all ingredients together until well mixed.

Yields 1 cup

Hot Wine Sauce

½ cup brown sugar
⅓ cup butter
½ cup port wine
½ tsp. nutmeg

1 Place wine and sugar in a saucepan on slow heat.

2 Add nutmeg and butter.

3 Pour over Christmas pudding.

Yields 1 cup

Mango Chutney

4 lb.	*green mango, peeled and cut off seed*
1½ lb.	*raisins*
1 oz.	*garlic*
1 oz.	*ground ginger*
2 tsp.	*salt*
3 pt.	*vinegar*
2 lb.	*brown sugar*
¼ tsp.	*scotch bonnet*

1. Dice the mango flesh.
2 Cut up the raisins.
3. Peel and chop the garlic.
4. Put all ingredients in a saucepan and simmer on low for about 2 hours stirring frequently. Cool and bottle.

Yields 12 cups

Hard Sauce

6 oz.	*icing sugar*
3 oz.	*butter*
2 tbsp.	*rum*

1 Cream butter and sugar until soft and fluffy.
2 Gradually beat in rum.
3 Use piping bag and rosette tip and pipe rosettes of hard sauce onto waxed paper and chill.
4 Remove and serve on servings of Christmas pudding as needed.

Yields 1 cup

White Sauce

Thin Sauce:

1 tbsp.	*butter*
1 cup	*milk*
1 tbsp.	*flour*
¼ tsp.	*salt*

Medium Sauce:

2 tbsp.	*butter*
1 cup	*milk*
2 tbsp.	*flour*
¼ tsp.	*salt*

Thick Sauce:

3 tbsp.	*butter*
1 cup	*milk*
3 tbsp.	*flour*
¼ tsp.	*salt*

1 Blend the melted butter and flour thoroughly (to make a blonde roux.)
2 Gradually add the cold milk while heating slowly.
3 Heat and stir constantly until smooth and thickened.
4 Cover over steam for 10 minutes longer then add salt.

Yields 1 cup

Cook's Tip

For a smooth sauce if the roux is hot, the milk should be cold and vice versa.

Soy Onion Sauce

¾ cup	*soy sauce*
1 tbsp.	*minced onion*
1 tbsp.	*oil*
¼ tsp.	*sugar*

1 Mix and set aside to blend flavours.

Yields 1 cup

THE BRICK OVEN

Making cakes is wonderful
There is one for every mood
Sometimes you make an angel cake
Sometimes its devils' food.

'Bake things' and most recipes were perfected in the brick oven or the iron dutch pot. A fine example of an old brick oven can be seen at Devon House in Kingston.

The mixture of flour, shortening, sugar, eggs and a leavening agent may vary but the propensity of Jamaican cooks to experiment and utilize ingredients at hand, produces many excellent 'bake things' which need not be sophisticated to be tasty such as the uncomplimentary 'toto' or the very simple but ever-popular 'bulla'.

Our spice buns are especially delicious. No Jamaican overseas would dream of celebrating Easter without an Easter bun from home and Christmas would not be complete without a taste of at least one Jamaican Christmas pudding.

1-2-3-4 Cake

Many people shy away from making a plain cake, because they are not sure it will turn out light and delicious. A few hints and a good recipe are all that are needed.

1 cup	*of butter (or 8 ozs.)*
2 cups	*of sugar*
4	*eggs*
1 tsp.	*vanilla*
3 cups	*of flour*
½ tsp.	*salt*
4 tsp.	*baking powder*
1 cup	*water*

1 Preheat oven at 375° F. for 15 minutes, Prepare two 8 or 9 inch layer tins, lining bottom with greaseproof paper. Grease paper but not sides of tin.

2 Cream butter and add sugar gradually. (Do not use butter at room temperature if room is warmer than 75° F. In Jamaica it is usually too soft at room temperature, so use about 10 minutes out of the refrigerator - not the freezer.)

3 Add eggs one at a time, beating each egg for about 3 minutes.

4 Add vanilla.

5 Sift flour, salt and baking powder. Add flour mixture and water alternately. Add flour in 4 portions and water in 3, beginning and ending with flour.

6 Pour in prepared layer tins.

7 Bake layers for 25 minutes. (If using 1 tin to bake mixture, lower temperature to 350° F. It will take approximately. 1¼ hours and will not be as light as cakes baked in layer tins.)

8 Allow cake to cool in pan 5-10 minutes. Turn out on wire rack to cool if icing separately. If you would like layers to stick together without using filling, as soon as they are turned out of the pan, put them together.

Serves 12

Coffee Cake

Some people expect coffee in coffee cake, but this crispy, crunchy coffee cake is an excellent 'go-with' for a steaming cup of Blue Mountain coffee.

Mix topping for coffee cake before mixing cake.

Topping:

½ cup	*brown sugar*
1 tbsp.	*flour*
1 tsp.	*cinnamon*
1 tbsp.	*melted butter*
½ cup	*broken nuts*

Cake:

¼ cup	*salad oil or melted shortening*
1	*beaten egg*
½ cup	*milk*
1½ cup	*sifted flour*
¾ cup	*sugar*
2 tsp.	*baking powder*
½ tsp.	*salt*

1 Combine brown sugar, flour, cinnamon, melted butter and ½ cup broken nuts for topping (almonds, walnuts etc.) Set aside.

2 Preheat oven to 375° F about 15 minutes.

3 Grease a 9 x 9 x 2 inch pan.

4 Combine salad oil, egg and milk.

5 Sift together dry ingredients.

6 Add milk mixture and mix with dry ingredients.

7 Pour into greased pan.

8 Sprinkle topping over batter and bake for about 25 minutes or until done.

9 Serve warm.

Serves 12

Carrot Cake

In the late 1980s, Carrot Cake was a popular dessert on local airlines.

1 lb.	*carrots, grated*
2 cups	*granulated sugar*
2 cups	*corn oil*
6	*eggs*
3 cups	*flour*
1 tsp.	*cloves*
1 tsp.	*ginger*
½ tsp.	*pimento*
½ tsp.	*salt*
2 tsp.	*baking powder*
1 tsp.	*baking soda*
1 cup	*nuts (walnuts preferred)*
1 cup	*mixed fruit*
1 cup	*raisins*
	vanilla/almond flavouring to taste

1. Preheat oven to 350° F. Grease 10 inch backup pan.
2. Mix all dry ingredients and sift.
3. Beat eggs, add oil and fold in.
4. Pour in baking pan and bake until done (about 1 hour.)

Serves 8

Cook's Tip

The residue of carrots after the drink is made, can make Carrot Cake but freshly grated carrot gives a much better taste.

Orange Cake for 50

Try your hand at baking a cake to serve 50 people.

1 lb.	*butter or margarine*
2 lb.	*sugar*
1¾ lb.	*sifted flour*
2 tbsp.	*baking powder*
9	*large eggs*
	rind of 1 orange
1 pt.	*water or milk*
1 tsp.	*salt*
	shortening

1. Prepare 18 x 12 x 2 ½ tin ahead of baking time. Grease lightly with shortening (unsalted butter.) Preheat oven to 350° F.
2. Cream butter and add sugar gradually.
3. Sift flour with baking powder and salt.
4. Add eggs one at a time and beat after each addition.
5. Add orange rind.
6. Add flour mixture in 4 portions alternately with milk or water (3 times) - begin and end with flour.
7. Pour into baking tin and bake at 350° F. for 45 minutes.
8. After taking cake from the oven allow it to stand in cake tin for 10 minutes before attempting to turn out on a cooling rack.
9. Cool well before applying frosting or icing.

Serves 50

Coffee Cake

Banana Cake

I got an S.O.S. for this recipe from a gentleman in Canada who attended a demonstration when I made this cake. After trying the recipe he told me the quantity was just right, the taste delicious, and that it should never be served without the sauce.

4 oz. *flour (1 cup)*
1 tsp. *baking powder*
¼ tsp. *baking soda*
¼ tsp. *salt*
1 *egg*
1 *ripe banana*
2 oz. *soft butter*
5 oz. *sugar*
½ tsp. *vanilla*

1 Preheat oven to 375° F.

2 Grease an 8 or 9 inch layer tin and dust with flour.

3 Sift flour, baking powder, baking soda and salt in a bowl.

4 In blender place egg, banana, butter sugar and vanilla and blend at maximum speed to a smooth consistency, approximately 1 minute.

5 Pour the liquidized mixture in the flour mixture and mix just long enough to combine thoroughly.

6 Pour into greased tin and bake for approximately 25 minutes.

7 Cool on a wire rack, and serve topped with banana cream.

Serves 6

Banana Cream
(for Banana Cake)

1 *ripe banana*
1 oz. *sugar*
¼ tsp. *nutmeg*
¼ pt. *cream, whipped and chilled (evaporated milk can be used.)*

1 Put banana, sugar and nutmeg in blender and blend until smooth.

2 Add to cream and serve with cake.

Cook's Tip
It is delicious served warm with cold cream.

Basic Sponge Cake

(Use for children's party, cakes for sponge flans, sponge fingers, ice box cakes etc.)

shortening
4 *eggs*
4 oz. *sugar (approximately)*
3 oz. *flour, sifted*
grated lemon rind

1 Preheat oven to 350° F.

2 Line an 8 or 9 inch baking tin with paper and grease with shortening.

3 Beat eggs and sugar until frothy.

4 Stir in the sifted flour with the lemon rind very lightly.

5 Half fill the tin.

6 Bake in a moderate oven until done and lightly coloured.

Serves 12

Cook's Tip
A little sugar sprinkled on top before baking gives a smooth crisp finish.

Ice Box Cake

1	*sponge cake (see recipe P. 102)*
½ lb.	*butter*
1 cup	*granulated sugar*
3	*eggs*
1 tsp.	*vanilla*
1 pt.	*whipping cream*
1 tbsp.	*sugar*
	cherries
	cracked nuts

1 Cream butter and sugar until smooth.

2 Add eggs, beating well after every addition.

3 Add vanilla.

4 Dampen a round, heavy bowl and line with strips of sponge cake, completely covering bottom and sides.

5 Pour half the filling in the bowl and lay more strips of cake over same.

6 Add rest of filling and again cover with strips of cake.

7 Fit a plate lightly inside bowl, so that it presses on the mixture (to mould cake.) Use a weight on top of plate in freezer at least overnight.

8 Unmould 1 hour before serving.

9 Whip 1 pt. cream with a tbsp. sugar and cover cake.

10 Decorate with cherries and cracked nuts.

Serves 12

Dundee Cake

If you would like to have a fruit cake with less fruits, but the same delicious taste, try this favourite of Mrs. Eleanor Jones. I have been specially asked to include the recipe for Dundee Cake in this cook-book.

5 oz.	*butter*
5 oz.	*granulated sugar*
3	*large eggs*
8 oz.	*plain flour*
1 tsp.	*baking powder*
6 oz.	*currants*
6 oz.	*raisins*
2 oz.	*glace cherries*
2 oz.	*candied peel, finely chopped*
2 tbsp.	*ground almonds*
2 oz.	*whole blanched almonds*
	grated rind of 1 small orange and 1 small lime
1dsp.	*milk*

1 Preheat oven to 325° F. for 15 minutes.

2 Line a 7 or 8 inch round baking tin with grease proof paper and grease.

3 Beat butter and sugar.

4 Whisk the eggs separately, then a little at a time, beat them into the creamed butter and sugar.

5 Using spatula fold in the flour and baking powder. If it seems too dry, add a dessert spoon of milk.

6 Fold in fruits and arrange almonds in circle on top.

7 Place in centre of the oven and bake for 2 to 2 ½ hours.

8 Cool in tin.

Yields one 9" cake

Pineapple Upside-down Cake

More suitable for dessert than tea.

1 tbsp.	*butter*
¼ cup	*brown sugar*
9	*canned pineapple slices*
9	*drained cherries*
1 ¼ cups	*sifted flour*
1 ½ tsp.	*baking powder*
¼ tsp.	*salt*
¼ cup	*shortening*
¾ cup	*granulated sugar*
2	*eggs beaten*
½ cup	*milk*
1 tsp.	*vanilla*

1 Grease bottom of frying pan with shortening and line with greaseproof paper.

2 Melt butter in pan at 220° F.

3 Sprinkle brown sugar over melted butter.

4 Arrange pineapple slices with cherries in centre of the slices and arrange over butter mixture. Set aside.

5 Sift together next 3 ingredients (flour, baking powder and salt.)

6 Beat shortening until creamy.

7 Add granulated sugar and continue beating.

8 Add eggs and beat well.

9 Add flour with milk and vanilla, stirring until smooth after each addition.

10 Spread on fruit.

11 Bake for 30 minutes. at 260° F.

12 Let stand for 5 minutes before turning out.

Serves 8

Cook's Tip

If using fresh pineapple slices, heat in light syrup (1 cup sugar, 2 cups water) before using. You can pour a cake mix over the pineapple mixture instead of starting from scratch.

Victoria Sandwich

This cake is one of the legacies of the British.

4 oz.	*butter or margarine*
4 oz.	*sifted flour*
1 tsp.	*baking powder*
4 oz.	*granulated sugar*
2	*large eggs, beaten*

1 Preheat oven to 325° F. for 15 minutes if using one tin, 375° F. if using layer tins.

2 Line and grease two 7 inch layer tins or one 9 inch tin.

3 Mix all ingredients in a bowl.

4 Beat with a wooden spoon for 2 to 3 minutes, until well mixed. (The mixture should then be lighter in colour and slightly glossy.)

5 Place in two 7 inch tins or one 9 inch tin.

6 Bake on the middle shelf for 25-35 minutes.

7 Turn out and cool on wire cooler.

8 If using two 7 inch tins, sandwich together with jam.

Yields one 9" cake

Black Forest Cake

If you have always wanted to make a black forest cake, here is an easy one.

3	*eggs*
3 oz.	*granulated sugar*
2 oz.	*plain flour*
1 oz.	*cocoa powder*
3 tbsp.	*kirsch*
1 pt.	*double or whipping cream*
	blackberry pie filling

Glace icing:

8 oz.	*icing sugar*
1 oz.	*cocoa powder*
2 tbsp.	*water*
	chocolate curls for decoration

1. Preheat oven to 350° F.
2. Line and grease 7 inch round cake tin.
3. Whisk the eggs and sugar until pale and thick.
4. Fold in flour and cocoa powder.
5. Pour the mixture into the lined and greased tin and bake for 40 minutes.
6. Cool on a wire rack.
7. Cut into 3 layers and soak each layer with 1 tablespoon kirsch.
8. Whip the cream until thick and sandwich the cake together with some of the cream and pie filling.
9. Pipe remaining cream on the side of the cake and a border on top.
10. Mix icing sugar, cocoa powder and water until smooth and pour over the top.
11. Decorate with chocolate curls

Yields one 7" cake

Chocolate Cake

4 oz.	*plain chocolate*
4 oz.	*flour*
1½ tsp.	*baking powder*
¼ tsp.	*baking soda*
	pinch of salt
4 oz.	*butter*
4 oz.	*granulated sugar*
4	*eggs (if large use 3)*

1. Preheat oven at 375° F.
2. Melt chocolate.Set aside.
3. Sift together flour, baking powder, baking soda and salt.
4. Cream butter well, gradually adding sugar.
5. Add softened chocolate to creamed mixture and beat well.
6. Add eggs, unbeaten, one at a time, adding a little flour with each to prevent curdling.
7. When all eggs have been added, mix in the remaining flour and beat for about 2 minutes.
8. Bake for 40 minutes.

Yields one 8" cake

Sweet Potato Pudding
(Two Pans)

Hell a top, Hell a bottom, Hallelujah in the middle!

This is a Jamaican riddle and most people know that the answer is a delicious, sweet potato pudding, baked in an iron dutch pot or dutch oven with live coals in the bottom of the coal stove and also on the top of the dutch pot. The pudding cooks at the top and at the bottom at the same time. This delicious hallelujah is best liked when the top, called 'sof pon top', is softer than the rest of the pudding. Winnie Risden-Hunter, Breakfast Club regular, loves this pudding hot, but you may also serve it cold.

2 lbs	*sweet potato, grated*
¼ lb.	*yam grated*
½ cup	*flour*
¼ lb.	*raisins*
1 tsp.	*baking powder*
½ tin	*evaporated milk*
5 cups	*coconut milk (2 coconuts)*
1 cup	*brown sugar*
2 tsp.	*vanilla*
½ tsp.	*nutmeg*
½ tsp.	*salt*
¼ cup	*sherry*
¼ cup	*rum*
1 oz.	*butter*

1 Preheat oven to 350° F

2 Mix grated potato, yam, flour, raisins and baking powder.

3 Mix evaporated milk, coconut, milk, sugar, vanilla, nutmeg, salt, sherry, rum and butter.

4 Pour milk mixture into potato mixture and beat until smooth.

5 Pour into a greased 9 inch pan.

6 Rest mixture about ½ hour.

7 Bake at 350° F about 1 - 1½ hours until centre is set.

8 Serve hot or cold.

Serves 12-16

Tie-A-leaf (front)
Sweet Potato Pudding (back)

Queen of Puddings

Mrs. Eulit Gayle said she felt like a queen whenever she served this pudding, especially in Nigeria where her husband was a training officer for civil servants and in Mexico where he was Charge d'Affaires in the Jamaican Embassy. It was also a favourite of her Jamaican friends.

	rind of 1 lemon, grated
1 pt.	*of cow's milk*
9	*slices of white bread (without crust)*
2 oz.	*butter*
¼ cup	*granulated sugar*
3	*eggs separated*
4 tbsp.	*jam*
3 tbsp.	*granulated sugar*

1 Preheat oven to 375° F

2 Put all ingredients in blender, except egg whites, jam and 3 tbsp. sugar.

3 Blend at maximum speed for 30 seconds.

4 Pour into a greased pie dish and bake at 375° F. for about 30 minutes or until set.

5 Take pudding out of the oven and spread the top with jam.

6 Make a meringue by whisking the egg whites until stiff, and gradually fold in 3 tbsp. of sugar.

7 Pile meringue mixture on top of jam.

8 Return to slow oven (300° F.) and bake until pale brown, about 10 minutes.

Serves 8

Cook's Tip

A mixer or whisk is better for making meringue. Make sure white is beaten enough, until stiff, before adding sugar. The blender is very useful but it cannot beat egg whites or cream butter and sugar.

Christmas Pudding and Cake

In Jamaica because there is never, ever a dream of a white Christmas, the pudding is never served hot. Consequently beef suet is hardly used in making Christmas puddings or mince pies. Most Jamaican housewives make one mixture and bake a portion for the cake and steam the remainder for the pudding. Raisins, currants and prunes are usually soaking for months or even years in real Jamaican rum, in anticipation of the delicious cake to be made the first week in December. This allows enough time for it to 'ripen' or mature for the yuletide season.

Preparing Fruits for Baking

Soak only raisins, currants and stoned prunes. If possible, grind all the prunes, half the raisins and half the currants, this will give the cake a 'bite'. Do not soak the dates, cherries, mixed peel or the nuts.

It is very important to wash the raisins and currants well. After washing, soak in cold water for half an hour, then lift the fruit from the soaking water and this will allow the sand to fall to the bottom of the vessel. Dry before adding rum. Spice may be added to the rum and wine but this is not a must.

To make a 9 inch pudding and a 9 inch cake, prepare and soak:

1 lb.	*raisins*
1 lb.	*currants*
1 lb.	*prunes*

1 Cover with a mixture of rum and port wine.

2 Soak in a glass jar with a tight-fitting lid. (Avoid using plastic containers when using rum.)

3 Before putting away, label the bottle, listing the quantities and the date.

4 From time to time, examine fruit in soak and add more rum and wine mixture as necessary, to keep the fruit covered.

Christmas Pudding

To make approximately 4 lb. of cake (enough to fill a 9 inch baking tin) follow this recipe.

½ lb.	*butter*
½ lb.	*granulated sugar*
1 tbsp.	*browning*
2 tsp.	*vanilla*
1 tsp.	*of almond flavouring*
2 tsp.	*lime juice*
1 tsp.	*lime or orange rind*
6	*eggs*
4 cups	*mixed fruits (raisins, currants, prunes, citron, cherries, dates)*
6 ozs.	*bread crumbs*
6 ozs.	*flour*
1 tsp.	*baking powder*
¼ tsp.	*salt*
1 tbsp.	*mixed spice*
1 cup	*white rum*
1 pt.	*port wine/brandy optional*
½ cup	*chopped nuts (not peanuts) optional*

1 Prepare tin by lining sides with 2 thicknesses of paper and the bottom with 4 thicknesses of brown paper and 1 of greaseproof paper.

2 Grease with shortening.

3 Beat butter and sugar until light and fluffy.

4 Mix in browning, vanilla and almond flavouring, lime juice and rind.

5 Add eggs one at a time and beat in well. Add soaked fruit, cherries, dates and nuts.

6 Mix breadcrumbs, flour, baking powder, salt and mixed spice.

7 Add alternately with rum and port wine.

8 Pour into prepared baking tins or steaming basins ¾ full.

9 Cover and make steaming basin watertight.

10 Place in steamer, or put over boiling water.

11 Continue to add boiling water until pudding steams, approximately 3 to 3 ½ hours. Cooking time varies with size of container.

12 Serve with hard sauce or hot wine sauce. (p. 97)

Yields one 9" pudding.

> **Cook's Tip**
> You may steam in the oven by setting baking tin in water or set a pan of boiling water below the pudding. Puddings can also be cooked in the pressure cooker.

Christmas Cake

Use the same ingredients as the recipe for Christmas pudding. Make one mixture and divide in two tins. Bake one tin and steam the other.

> **Cook's Tip**
> Christmas cakes and puddings can be made up to 4 weeks before serving as they actually improve with age. I use granulated sugar instead of brown sugar because it creams quicker. Always taste browning before adding to mixture as sometimes it can be very salty. Draining off liquid from fruits, allows the cook to be better able to judge the amount of liquid added to mixture. Toast nuts and cool before adding to cake mixture.

Bread Pudding

Most men seem to like to cook bread pudding, and this recipe is a never fail one.

10	*slices white bread*
2 qt.	*cow's milk*
1 tin	*evaporated milk*
5	*eggs*
2 cups	*granulated sugar*
1 tsp.	*nutmeg*
1 tsp.	*vanilla*
½ cup	*rum*
½ cup	*sherry*
½ tsp.	*salt*

1 Heat oven 350° F.

2 Grease a 3 qt. ovenproof glass dish with butter.

3 Remove the crust from slices of bread, butter bread cut in cubes and place in greased dish.

4 Heat milk, cool and mix with all other ingredients.

5 Pour milk mixture over bread cubes.

6 Allow to rest for 15 minutes before baking.

7 Place ovenproof dish in larger container in ½ to 1 inch boiling water.

8 Bake for 45 minutes.

9 Take out while still soft.

10 Serve warm.

Serves 12

> **Cook's Tip**
> Resting pudding for 15 minutes or more helps the bread to absorb the custard.

Coconut Pudding

½ cup grated coconut
¼ cup bread crumbs
½ pt. milk
2 eggs
1 oz. butter
2 tbsp. granulated sugar
pinch of salt

1 Preheat oven to 350° F. for 15 minutes.

2 Put all ingredients in a blender and beat until smooth.

3 Bake in a buttered pie dish for 1 hour.

Serves 6

Brownie Pudding

1 cup sifted all purpose flour
¾ cup granulated sugar
2 tbsp. cocoa
2 tsp. baking powder
½ tsp. salt
½ cup milk
2 tbsp. salad oil or melted shortening
1 tsp. vanilla
¾ -1 cup chopped walnuts
¾ cup brown sugar
¼ cup cocoa
1¾ cups hot water

1 Preheat oven to 350° F.

2 Sift together first 5 ingredients (i.e. flour, sugar, cocoa, baking powder and salt.)

3 Add milk, salad oil and vanilla to first set of ingredients.

4 Mix together until smooth.

5 Pour into greased 8 x 8 x 2 inch pan.

6 Mix together brown sugar, ¼ cup cocoa, walnuts and hot water.

7 Pour over pudding batter.

8 Bake for about 45 minutes.

Serves 8

Coconut Totoes

If you are told that your plain cake is like toto, it is not a compliment. But toto is sought after, especially in these days when totoes are no longer easily available from small bakers. Get nostalgic and make a batch of totoes for the family.

¼ lb. butter
1 cup granulated sugar
2 cups flour
2 tsp. baking powder
1 tsp. cinnamon
¼ tsp. nutmeg
Pinch of pimento (allspice)
2 cups grated dry coconut
2 tsp. vanilla
1 egg beaten
approximately ½ cup milk

1 Grease shallow baking tin and preheat oven to 400° F.

2 Cream butter and sugar.

3 Sieve together flour, baking powder, coconut, cinnamon, nutmeg, and pimento. Add to butter and sugar mixture.

4 Add vanilla, beaten egg and just enough milk to mix to a stiff dough.

5 Spread evenly in greased shallow baking tin.

6 Bake for roughly 30 minutes.

7 Cut into 12 squares.

Yields 12

Bullas

These inexpensive, flat, circular cakes are a favourite of Jamaicans. They are difficult to spoil and there are almost as many recipes as cooks (rivalled only by the different kinds of ovens in which they are baked.)

8 oz.	*new sugar (wet sugar)*
	or
10 oz.	*very dark sugar with just enough water to blend sugar in a thick syrup (about 2 oz.)*
3 cups	*flour*
1 tsp.	*baking powder*
½ tsp.	*baking soda*
¼ tsp.	*salt*
1 tsp.	*cinammon*
¼ tsp.	*nutmeg*
½ tsp.	*ground ginger*
½ tsp.	*pimento*
2 tbsp.	*melted butter*

1. Lightly grease and flour baking sheet and preheat oven to 400° F.
2. Make a syrup of water and sugar, if not using wet sugar.
3. Sift together dry ingredients and make a well in centre.
4. Pour the thick syrup and melted butter or margarine into centre and blend all together lightly.
5. Turn out on well floured board and knead for a few minutes, roll out to a thickness of ¼ inch or just a bit thicker.
6. Cut circles with biscuit cutter or use a drinking glass to cut circles.
7. Raise bullas with a well floured spatula and place on baking sheet.
8. Bake for 20 minutes.

Yields 12 bullas

Rock Buns

This is an easy recipe with which to start boys and girls cooking.

½ lb.	*flour*
1 tsp.	*baking powder*
3 oz.	*sugar*
3 oz.	*margarine*
1	*egg*
2 oz.	*currants or raisins (optional)*
	enough milk to mix a stiff dough

1. Grease baking tray and preheat oven to 400° F.
2. Add baking powder and sugar to flour.
3. Chop, flake and rub margarine into flour.
4. Add currants and raisins.
5. Add enough milk to mix to a very stiff dough.
6. Add egg.
7. Spoon in rough heaps on a greased baking tray and bake for about 10-15 minutes.

Yields 12 buns.

Cook's Tip

1 oz. of grated coconut may be added to mixture for tasty cookies.

Tie-a-Leaf
(Duckoono, Boyo or Blue Drawers)

Many people think they will not be able to make this dish, because they have no leaf to tie it in, nor any banana bark to tie it with. Please know that the taste is just as good tied in foil with a string. Call it Duckoono, Boyo or Blue Drawers, this West African dish is always popular. Tie-a-leaf is like a boiled pudding and can be made with cornmeal, green bananas and sweet potatoes or a mixture of your choice. Grated coconut is always included to give a 'bite' that is appreciated.

3 cups grated green bananas
2 cups grated sweet potatoes
1 cup flour
1 tsp. baking powder
1 tsp. salt
2 cups coconut milk
1½ cups brown sugar
1 tsp. vanilla
1 tsp. mixed spice
2 tbsp. melted margarine
1 cup grated coconut
¼ cups raisins

1 Combine grated bananas, sweet potatoes, flour, baking powder, salt, mixed spice, margarine, grated coconut and raisins .

2 Sweeten coconut milk with sugar and add vanilla.

3 Pour milk mixture in banana mixture and blend well.

4 Prepare banana leaf by cutting off centre vein and holding leaf over boiling water or before an open flame to make it pliable.

5 Put ½ cup mixture in banana leaves or in foil and fold up sides to make parcel.

6 Tie with banana bark or twine.

7 Place parcels in enough boiling water to cover and boil for 30 minutes.

8 Remove leaf covering to serve or could be placed on a small piece of prepared banana leaf and garnished with nuts and chilled banana cream.

Serves 8

Cook's Tip

1 lb. cornmeal could be used instead of green bananas and sweet potatoes and cooked for 45 minutes.

Currant Cookies

These cookies were served at a bridge game one morning. They were so delicious, I asked the hostess for the recipe and she graciously gave it to me. I have used it often and therefore happily pass on the recipe for your enjoyment. Happy munching!

3 cups flour
1 cup sugar
5 tsp. baking flour
1 cup currants
1 cup margarine (8 oz.)
1 egg
1 cup milk

1 Preheat oven to 375° F.

2 Mix all dry ingredients.

3 Put in margarine and add milk and eggs.

4 Drop in spoonfuls on greased cookie sheet.

5 Bake for 15 to 20 minutes.

Yields 28 or 50 smaller cookies (depending on the size of the spoon used to drop the mixture)

Buns

Jamaican buns are becoming very popular all over the world. Most overseas graduates of the University of the West Indies confess that their addiction to saturday night bun and cheese is still with them, and they readily acknowledge the part it played in their obtaining a degree. Bun and cheese is the traditional fare for Easter. All the supermarkets are stocked with different sizes, quality and prices. The Post offices and even the airports have their fair share of parcels with buns for absent relatives. Many housewives, however, like to try their hand at making buns for their families each with a preference for the raising agent, so here are four recipes using Yeast, Baking powder, Baking soda and Stout. Try all four and enjoy!

Easter Spice Bun
(Baking Soda)

2 cups	*brown sugar*
2 cups	*hot water*
3 tbsp.	*margarine*
½ tsp.	*salt*
1 tsp.	*cinnamon*
½ tsp.	*nutmeg*
¼ tsp.	*ground cloves*
1 lb.	*raisins*
1 tbsp.	*baking soda*
3 cups	*flour*

1 Preheat oven to 350° F.

2 In a saucepan, bring to the boil brown sugar, hot water, margarine, salt, cinnamon, nutmeg, cloves, raisins. Simmer for 15 minutes and cool.

3 Sift together baking soda and flour.

4 Add cold mixture to flour.

5 Bake in a greased tin until done (about 1 - 1½ hours.)

Yields 1 loaf

Easter Spice Bun
(Baking Powder)

This recipe is a favourite of my niece, Ditty Tapper, in Los Angeles. Whenever there is a Jamaican function, Ditty is sure to have a request for it. After making this bun and tasting it, you will know why.

3 cups	*flour*
4 tsp.	*baking powder*
1 tsp.	*nutmeg*
1 tsp.	*cinnamon*
2 cups	*brown sugar*
1	*egg*
1 cup	*milk or wine*
1 cup	*raisins*
1 tbsp.	*butter*
1 tsp.	*lime juice*
	Pinch of salt

1 Preheat oven to 350° F. about 15 minutes.

2 Beat egg. Add sugar, then melted butter and 1 cup milk or wine.

3 Pour into dry ingredients and beat until smooth.

4 Add raisins.

5 Pour into lined and greased loaf tin and bake for approximately 1 hour.

6 As soon as bun is done, make a glaze using ½ cup brown sugar and ½ cup water, boil until thick, spread on bun and pop back in oven for about 5 minutes.

Yields 1 loaf

Easter Bun

Easter Spice Bun
(Yeast)

Many people are afraid of using yeast because they are not sure of what temperature to use. There is no magic to cooking with yeast. Yeast cakes (now almost absent from supermarket shelves) take a lower temperature (110° F) than dried yeast, which works well at 115° F. A candy thermometer will take all the guesswork out of cooking when making breads, buns, candies, jellies, yoghurt etc. an investment you would be glad you made. This recipe is a very old one, and if followed carefully will make 7 delicious 8 x 4 buns.

3½ lb.	*flour*
2	*packs yeast*
1 lb.	*brown sugar*
3½ pt.	*milk or milk and water*
12 oz.	*margarine*
1½-2 lb	*mixed fruits (cherries, citron, raisins, currants, prunes, mixed peel)*
½ pt.	*new sugar (can substitute ½ lb. more of brown sugar)*
8 oz.	*grated cheddar cheese*
3	*eggs*
3 tbsp.	*mixed spice (cinnamon, nutmeg, mace)*
1 tsp.	*caraway seeds*
2 tbsp.	*vanilla*

1 Line tins with grease paper and grease well.

2 Preheat oven to 400° F.

3 Sift the flour into a warm bowl.

4 Cream the yeast with a teaspoon of sugar and add the milk 115° F. warm.

5 Add to 1 lb. of flour gradually, stirring to make a smooth batter.

6 Cover with a clean cloth and set to rise in a warm place for 1½ to 2 hours until double in bulk.

7 Rub the margarine into remaining flour.

8 Prepare the fruits and mix with the dry ingredients.

9 When yeast mixture has doubled in bulk (about 2 hours) combine with all the other ingredients and mix until smooth.

10 Shape as required and place in a well greased loaf tin. Rub bits of batter in a little flour to make twists of dough and use to decorate. Allow to rise.

11 Bake at 400° F. for the first 10 minutes. Reduce heat to 325°F and cook until done.

12 Make a glaze by boiling 1 cup brown sugar and 1 cup water until thick and brush the bun with the glaze, immediately it comes out of the oven.

Yields 7 spice buns.

Easter Spice Bun
(Stout)

1½ cups	*brown sugar*
2 dsp.	*melted butter*
2 tsp.	*golden syrup or honey*
2 tsp.	*mixed spice*
1 cup	*stout*
3 cups	*flour*
3 tsp.	*baking powder*
1 cup	*mixed fruits*
1 or 2	*eggs (if eggs are small use 2)*

1 Preheat oven to 400° F.

2 Dissolve sugar, butter, syrup and spices in stout on low heat.

3 Mix flour baking powder and fruit.

4 Beat eggs and mix all ingredients together.

5 Put in greased and lined tin.

6 Bake for approximately 1 hour.

Yields 1 loaf

Banana Bread

In Jamaica, Banana cake and Banana bread are synonymous but this does not detract from the delicous morsel this recipe can produce for 6 portions.

¼ lb.	*butter*
1 cup	*granulated sugar*
1	*egg beaten*
3	*large ripe bananas crushed*
2 cups	*of flour*
2 tsp.	*baking powder*
1 tsp.	*baking soda*
1 tsp.	*cinnamon*
¼ tsp.	*nutmeg*
	pinch of salt
½ cup	*milk*
2 tsp.	*vanilla*
¼ cup	*raisins*

1. Cream butter and sugar.
2. Add egg to butter and sugar.
3. Add crushed bananas and mix well.
4. Sift flour, baking powder, baking soda, cinnamon, nutmeg and salt.
5. Add flour mixture to butter, sugar and egg mixture along with milk and vanilla.
6. Add raisins.
7. Pour into greased and lined loaf tin and bake at 350° F. for 1 hour or until done.

Serves 6

Cook's Tip

Most breads and cakes made with fresh fruit use both baking powder and baking

Corn Bread

Here is a very easy recipe for a popular quick bread.

1¼ cups	*flour*
¾ cups	*cornmeal*
¼ cup	*sugar*
4½ tsp.	*baking powder*
½ tsp.	*salt*
1	*egg beaten*
⅔ cups	*milk*
⅓ cup	*melted margarine*

1 Preheat oven 425° F for approximately 15 minutes.

2 Grease loaf tin (8 x 4).

3 Sift dry ingredients.

4 Mix together well-beaten egg, with milk and melted margarine.

5 Pour milk mixture in dry ingredients. Do not over mix, as this may cause tunnels.

6 Pour in greased loaf tin, and bake for approximately 30 minutes.

8 Serve hot.

Serves 6

SUGAR AND SPICE

To say that most Jamaicans have a sweet tooth is an understatement. This seems to have been a recognized fact from the time of the second World War when Jamaican airmen got extra rations of sugar, rum and coffee, courtesy of the Colonial office.

Most of our pastries and desserts are based on our wide variety of tropical fruits. Fruits are often eaten fresh from the tree, especially mangoes. The mango walk, as a mango grove is called, is not always easy for walking, since most pickers reject and eat on the site.

Today we adopt a more formal way of using the new varieties of table mangoes that are now being grown and like all our fruits they are eaten chilled or canned, made into ices or combined with milk and sugar or sugar and lime or with that favourite of Jamaicans - sweetened condensed milk.

Plantains, bananas, coconuts, guavas, tamarinds and otaheite apples,to name just a few, are stewed and used creatively in a variety of delicious tarts and pies, trifles, and sweets. Who can resist a slice of otaheite apple pie, a sugary, chewy coconut gizzada, a slice of guava cheese or some sweet, sweet tamarind balls?

No-bake Cheesecake

Mix this delicious, tender, creamy cheesecake in 20 minutes. Pop into the refrigerator for two to three hours and presto! - it's ready.

Crumb mixture:

3 tbsp.	*melted butter*
¾ cup	*cracker crumbs*
2 tbsp.	*sugar*
¼ tsp.	*cinnamon*
¼ tsp.	*nutmeg*

Filling:

3	*envelopes unflavoured gelatine*
1 cup	*milk*
2	*eggs separated*
3 cups	*(24 oz.) creamed cottage cheese*
3 oz.	*frozen orange juice*
3 oz.	*frozen lime juice*
¼ cup	*granulated sugar*
1 cup	*heavy cream whipped*

1 Grease an 8 or 9 inch spring form pan lightly so that wax paper cut to fit will cling to bottom of pan (if spring form pan is not available use loaf or square pan that holds 8 cups.)

2 Combine all the ingredients of the crumb mixture.

3 Press ½ cup of the crumb mixture into the pan.

4 To un-mould, invert on serving plate. Remove wax paper.

To make filling:

1 Dust gelatine on milk in a 2½ qt. saucepan.

2 Add egg yolks, stir well.

3 Place over low heat, stirring constantly until gelatine dissolves and mixture thickens slightly for 2 to 3 minutes.

4 Remove from heat.

5 Sieve or beat cottage cheese (in small bowl or electric mixer on high speed) 3 to 4 minutes.

6 Stir cottage cheese with frozen orange juice and lime juice into gelatine mixture. Wash bowl and beaters (fat left on beaters will prevent egg whites from whipping.)

7 Beat egg whites until stiff, gradually add sugar and beat until very stiff.

8 Fold into gelatine mixture, fold in whipped cream.

9 Turn into prepared pan, sprinkle with reserved crumb mixture.

10 Chill until firm, 2 to 3 hours.

Serves 8-12

Cheese Cake

This cheesecake is not only easy, it is scrumptious and will make a delicious dessert for 12 people.

½ cup	*Graham cracker crumbs (local whole wheat biscuits can be used)*
2 lb.	*cream cheese (four 8 oz. packs used at room temperature)*
1 ¾	*cups sugar*
	juice and grated rind of one lemon
1 tsp.	*vanilla*
4	*eggs*

1 Preheat oven to 250° F.

2 Butter one 8 x 3 inch cake pan and sprinkle with Graham cracker crumbs.

3 Set pan aside.

4 Place cream cheese, sugar, lemon juice, lemon rind and vanilla in large bowl of mixer and beat at low speed.

5 Add eggs one at a time and gradually increase speed to high.

6 Continue beating until mixture is smooth.

7 Pour and scrape batter into the prepared pan and shake gently to level mixture.

8 Set the pan inside a slightly larger pan and pour boiling water into the outer pan to a depth of ½ inch. Do not let edge of cheesecake pan touch rim of larger pan.

9 Bake at 250° F. for 90 minutes. Increase to 275° F for 30 minutes. more.

10 Turn off heat and let cake set in oven for 1 hour.

11 Lift cake out of the water bath and place on a rack. Let stand 2 hours.

12 Invert serving plate over cake and carefully turn upside down so that cake comes out crumb side up.

13 Garnish with fruit. Can be frozen.

Serves 12

Lemon Ice Box Pie

Prior to 1950 all refrigerators came with a handy use and care booklet and several recipes. These were new to the housewife. One such recipe was lemon icebox pie. I think the recipes in the booklets sold the refrigerators more than the dealers imagined. This recipe lived in Trixie Bucknor's booklet.

Spice Crumb Crust:

¾ cup *bread crumbs or biscuit crumbs*
⅓ cup *brown sugar*
½ tsp. *nutmeg*
1 tsp. *mixed spice (cinnamon, cloves, mace)*
2 tbsp. *melted butter*

Filling:

1 *can evaporated milk*
2 *eggs*
½ cup *sugar*
⅓ cup *lemon juice (we used ½ lime and ½ orange)*
1 tsp. *lemon peel*

1 Mix bread or biscuit crumbs, brown sugar, nutmeg and mixed spice with melted butter.

2 Put in metal ice cube tray without divider or suitable container and pat with the back of a spoon.

3 Put in freezer until ready to put in filling.

To make filling:

1 Leave evaporated milk in tin and put in freezer overnight.

2 Next day, separate eggs.

3 Beat yolks and mix with sugar, juice and peel.

4 Beat egg whites stiff, then lightly fold in yolk mixture.

5 Turn frozen evaporated milk into bowl and beat until stiff.

6 Carefully fold into egg mixture.

7 Pour into ice tray on top spice crumbs.

8 Decorate with nuts and cherries.

Serves 6

Surprise Pastry Packages

Here is a never-fail pastry I know you will enjoy making and eating. Use either recipe below:

Pastry:

1 cup *butter*
8 oz. *cream cheese*
2 cups *flour*

1 Preheat oven to 375° F.

2 Combine all ingredients until they form a dough. (This can be done in a food processor.)

3 Divide the dough into 4 balls.

4 Flour a rolling pin and board.

5 Pat balls into circles and roll thin.Trim the dough into a circle.

Recipe #1 (sweet)

1 Spread with jam, nuts, mini chocolate chips, sugar and cinnamon (any combination or single sweet ingredient.)

2 Cut the circles into pizza wedges.

3 Roll up each wedge, starting with the large end.

4 Bake on lightly-greased cookie sheet for about 15 minutes. or until lightly browned.

Recipe #2 (savoury):

1 In centre of dough circles place a teaspoonful of a cooked meat, cooked vegetables or cheese filling.

2 Fold over half of the dough to form a tart.

3 Press around edge with a fork.

4 Bake about 15 minutes. on lightly greased cookie sheet.

Queen of Pudding (Following page Left) (front)
Otaheite Apple Pie (Following page Left)
Plantain Tarts (Following page Right) (front and left)
Ripe Banana Fritters (Following page Right)

Cook's Tip

Either recipe can be made ahead of time and kept in the refrigerator. The balls of dough can be wrapped in foil and kept in the refrigerator for a week. Left-over dough can be rolled out, cut out with cookie cutters, sprinkled with sugar and baked for sugar cookies (350° F. for about 12 minutes.)

Otaheite Apple Pie

Otaheite apples make a delicious pie. They can be used fresh or stewed. They also freeze well when stewed and will allow you to enjoy this pie out of the apple season.

6 *Otaheite apples*
1 cup *sugar*
½ tsp. *salt*

1 Preheat oven to 400° F.

2 Do not peel apples but cut and discard seeds.

3 Rough chop and cover with water.

4 Add sugar and salt.

5 Boil mixture until apples are almost transparent.

6 Pour into prepared pie shell and cover with pastry.

7 Make some slits in top of pastry to allow steam to escape.

8 Bake at 400° F. for 10 minutes. and then reduce heat to 350° F. until pastry is cooked (about another 30 minutes.)

Serves 6

Cook's Tip

Can be served warm with vanilla ice cream for a hearty dessert.

Coconut Gizzada
(pinch-me-round)

This coconut tart is well liked, but most persons use a different recipe, although the method is similar. A mixture of grated coconut and sugar is put in a pastry shell.

Pastry:

2 cups	*flour*
½ tsp.	*salt*
2½ oz.	*butter or margarine*
1½ oz.	*shortening*
¼ cup	*ice water*

Filling:

1	*large coconut, grated*
1 cup	*light brown sugar*
¼ tsp.	*grated nutmeg*
1 tbsp.	*water*
1 tbsp.	*butter*

1 Preheat oven to 350° F.

2 Sift flour and salt for pastry shells. Add butter and shortening and cut in flour. Pour in ice water to form a dough.

3 With a pastry blender, two knives, or fingers, blend until mixture resembles coarse crumbs.

4 With hands, shape into a ball and wrap in foil, waxed paper or plastic.

5 Allow to rest in refrigerator for 30 minutes. (not the freezer.)

6 Divide pastry in 8 pieces.

7 With hands roll each piece of pastry into a ball then use a rolling pin to roll balls flat to make a 3 inch circle ¼ inch thick.

8 Pinch edges to form a ridge to hold in coconut and sugar mixture.

9 Put on greased tin sheets and partly bake shells.

To make filling:

1 Mix coconut, sugar, nutmeg and water and cook over a low flame for about 20 minutes.

2 Add butter.

3 Fill shells with coconut mixture and bake for a further 15-20 minutes.

Yields 8

Ripe Banana Fritters

If you can count to 1, you will remember the ingredients for these banana fritters.

1	*ripe banana*
1 tbsp.	*sugar*
1	*egg*
½ tsp.	*vanilla*
½	*nutmeg*
1 tsp.	*baking powder*
1 tbsp	*flour*
	pinch of salt
	oil for frying

1 Crush ripe banana and add sugar.

2 Add egg, vanilla and nutmeg.

3 Mix baking powder, salt and flour and add to banana mixture.

4 Drop by tablespoon and fry in oil or on a hot griddle.

5 Drain on paper towelling and sprinkle with granulated sugar.

Yields 10

Plantain Tarts

Pastry:

2 cups *sifted flour*
½ tsp. *salt*
1 cup *vegetable shortening*
2-4 tbsp. *iced water*

Filling:

1 cup *ripe plantain, peeled and cut up*
¼ cup *sugar*
¼ cup *water*
½ tsp. *nutmeg*
1 tbsp. *raisins*
1 tbsp. *butter*
1 tsp. *vanilla*
pastry (see p. 121 for method)
red food colouring (optional)

1 Preheat oven to 450° F.

2 In saucepan combine plantain, sugar, and water.

3 Cook over low heat until plantain is cooked.

4 Remove from heat and add nutmeg, vanilla, raisins and butter and a little red food colouring if used.

5 Allow filling to cool before filling tart.

To make pastry:

1 Combine flour and salt with shortening and cut in with pastry blender until flaky. Add ice water to bind together, form in a ball, wrap and refrigerate.

2 Roll out dough on lightly floured board about ⅛ inch in thickness.

3 Cut 4 inch rounds, or larger.

4 Spoon cooled filling in the centre of each 4 inch round, fold over and seal with crimper or the prongs of a fork.

5 Place tarts on a baking sheet.

6 Brush tops with a little milk and prick top with a fork.

7 Bake at 450° F. for 10 minutes. and reduce heat to 350° F. and bake for a further 25 to 30 minutes. Pastry should be delicately brown.

Serves 6

Cook's Tip

Red food colouring and raisins are both optional.

Baked Bananas

6 *ripe bananas*
6 tbsp. *brown sugar*
2 oz. *butter*
1 cup *orange juice*

1 Grease ovenproof dish to hold the amount of bananas required.

2 Peel bananas and sprinkle with 1 tablespoon sugar for each banana.

3 Pour enough orange juice or milk to come half way up the side of the dish.

4 Dot with butter.

5 Bake at 350° F. for 20 minutes.

6 Serve warm or cold with chilled cream, chilled evaporated milk or delicious chilled coconut cream.

Serves 3

Crepe Suzettes

Most of these ingredients you will quite likely have on hand. Crepes freeze well, so do them ahead of time and use as required. I always remember Mrs. Alfred Rattray, wife of a former Ambassador to Washington, whenever I make this easy and delicious recipe. She gave me a crepe recipe book and crepe pan.

It is always easier to make the orange butter sauce before making the crepes.

Sauce:

	rind of ½ orange
½ cup	*orange juice*
2 tbsp.	*lemon juice*

or

1 tbsp.	*orange juice and*
1 tbsp.	*lime juice*
½ cup	*(4 oz.) soft butter*
1 cup	*(8 oz.) sugar*

Crepes:

	rind of 1 orange
1 cup	*milk*
3	*eggs*
½ cup	*sifted cake flour*
1 tbsp.	*sugar*
¼ tsp.	*salt*

To make sauce:

1. Blend orange juice, lemon juice and rind for 2 minutes in electric blender.
2. Add butter and sugar, blend for another 2 minutes.

   Yields 1½ cups of sauce.

To make crepes:

1. Place milk and orange rind in the electric blender.
2. Blend until rind looks grated. Add remaining ingredients and blend until smooth - about 30 seconds.
3. Fry the pancakes thin, using ¼ cup batter for each pancake.Cook until lightly browned on one side, turn and cook other side until also lightly browned.
4. As each pancake is done, spread with orange butter sauce and roll up.

   Serves 4-6

Coconut Creme

After a heavy meal, serve a light dessert like coconut creme. It can be made the day before and set in individual dessert dishes for ease of serving. Older wide champage glasses can come in handy here.

1 pt.	*thick coconut milk*
1 tbsp.	*unflavoured gelatine*
1 tin	*sweetened condensed milk*
¼ tsp.	*grated nutmeg*
	pinch of salt
1 pt.	*water*

1. Sprinkle gelatine on ½ cup of coconut milk.
2. When soft, melt on a low flame and add to the remaining milk.
3. Sweeten with condensed milk and add salt.
4. Strain and put in dessert dishes.
5. Sprinkle grated nutmeg and chill. Decorate and serve.

   Serves 6

Grater Cake

Use either recipe below.

Recipe #1

2 cups *grated coconut*
3 cups *granulated sugar*
½ cup *water*
pinch of salt

Recipe #2

2 cups *grated coconut*
1 lb. *of brown sugar*
½ cup *water*
½ tsp. *ginger*
pinch of salt

1 Combine all ingredients in a thick bottomed saucepan.

2 Boil until coconut is cooked and the liquid dries up and the mixture is sticky enough to hold together.

3 Remove from heat and beat mixture for 2 or 3 minutes.

4 Drop on to a greased tray or mixture can be poured into a square dish 8 x 8 x 2 and pressed with the back of spoon. (For recipe #2 shape into cakes or balls while still hot and allow to cool.) When cool cut with a knife into squares.

5 A second batch may be made and coloured pink and placed on top of the first mixture which is white.

Yields 10-12

Instant Coconut Ice Cream

Try this instant ice cream with the harder jelly from coconuts.

jelly from 1 coconut (not too hard, not too soft)
3 tbsp. *granulated sugar*
3 tbsp. *powdered milk*
about 8 ice cubes (refrigerator cubes)

1 Blend coconut jelly, sugar and powdered milk together.

2 Continue blending, adding enough ice cubes until creamy.

3 Serve immediately.

Serves 6

Refrigerator Orange Ice Cream

Here is an easy, delicious and inexpensive dessert.

1 *orange (juiced and strained)*
3 tbsp. *granulated sugar*
1 *14 oz. can evaporated milk*
pinch of salt
1 tsp. *vanilla*
2 *eggs, beaten*

1 Sweeten orange juice with sugar.

2 Add 3 ice cubes.

3 Pour evaporated milk on ice cubes in orange juice.

4 Add salt, vanilla and beaten eggs.

5 Pour in metal ice cube tray without divider or any suitable container and set in freezer.

6 When set, remove and beat in chilled mixer bowl with chilled beaters.

7 Return to freezer and allow to set firm.

Serves 6

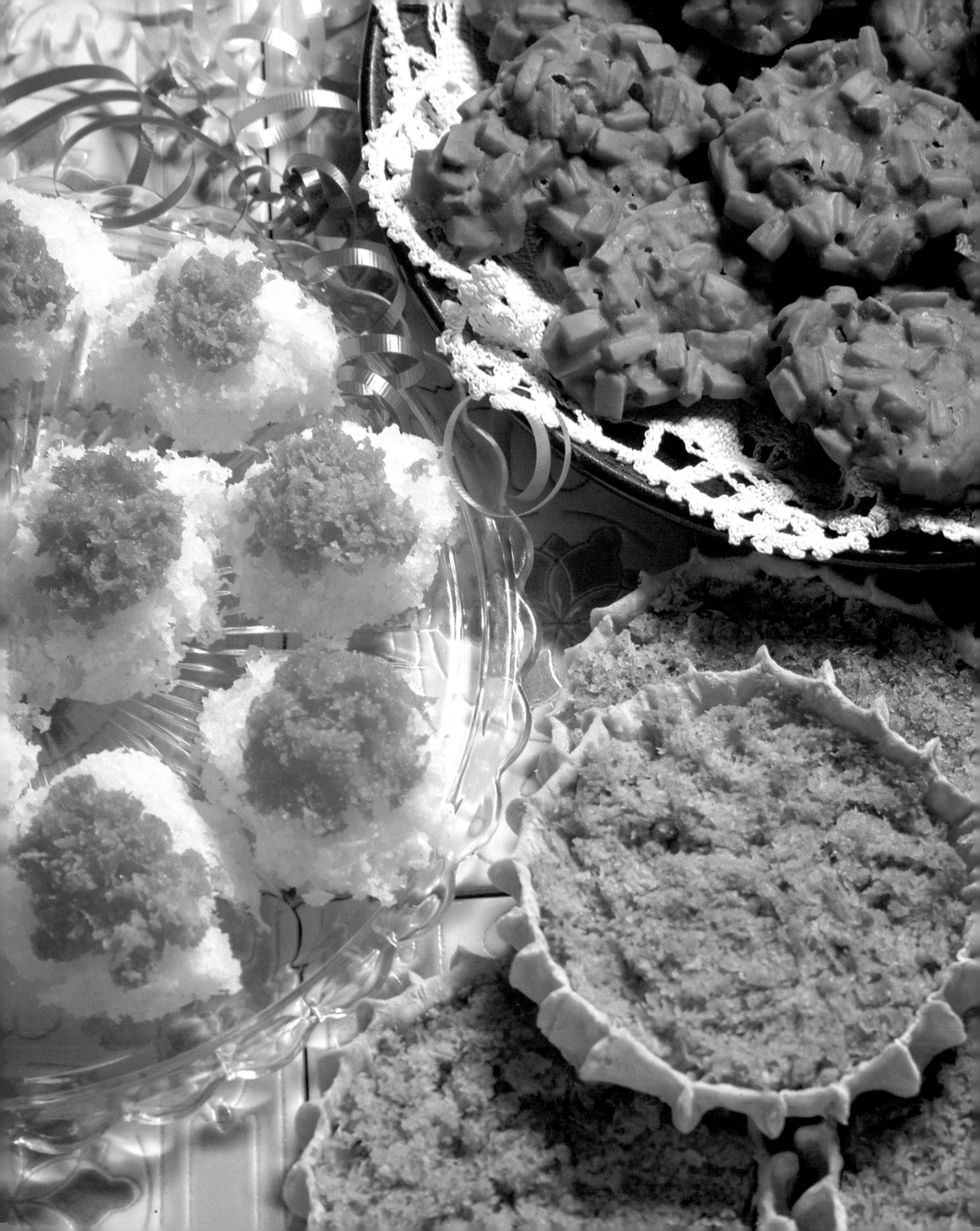

Pawpaw Sherbet

Have all ingredients ready but do not mix until ready to serve.

1 lb.	*pawpaw, peeled and diced*
½ cup	*condensed milk*
1 tsp.	*vanilla*
½ tsp.	*nutmeg*
1	*tray ice cubes*

1 In blender jar put pawpaw, condensed milk, vanilla and nutmeg.

2 Blend at high speed for 30 seconds.

3 Add 3 ice cubes and blend again.

4 Continue adding ice cubes in threes.

5 Blend until creamy and serve immediately.

Serves 6

Coconut Drops

One of the first fast foods sold at the school gate. Popular whether you call it drops or chip-chip or cut cake.

2 cups	*diced coconut*
1 tsp.	*powdered ginger or*
1 tbsp.	*grated root ginger*
1 tsp.	*vanilla*
1 lb.	*brown sugar*
1	*pinch salt*

1 Combine all ingredients adding sufficient water to cook coconut (about ½-¾ cup.)

2 Boil until very sticky (about 20-30 minutes.)

3 Beat a little and drop by spoonfuls onto a greased tin sheet.

Yields 12

Coconut Gizzada (Previous page Left) (front)
Coconut Drops (Previous page Left) (back)
Grater Cake (Previous page Right) (left)
Grapefruit Delight (Previous page Right)

Creme Caramel

Caramel:

½ cup	*granulated sugar*

Custard filling:

1 cup	*milk*
4	*eggs*
1 tin	*condensed milk*
1 tin	*evaporated milk*
1 tsp.	*vanilla*
	grated nutmeg
1 tbsp.	*rum or sherry*

1 Heat ½ cup granulated sugar slowly in a small saucepan until golden brown. Melt the sugar over a moderate heat. Cook caramel in about a ¼ cup of water.

2 Pour caramel in individual ovenproof custard cups and allow to set.

To make custard:

1 Heat 1 cup milk.

2 Beat egg yolks and mix with condensed and evaporated milk.

3 Add heated milk, vanilla and rum or sherry to the egg mixture, return to saucepan and cook gently over a very low heat stirring continuously, until custard has thickened enough to coat a spoon.

4 Strain custard mixture over caramel. Sprinkle nutmeg over custard.

5 Place in a shallow ovenproof dish. Fill dish with boiling water halfway up to the custard cups (about ½ inch of water). Bake for approximately 30 minutes.

6 Can be served warm or cool. Turn into a dessert dish so that the caramel sauce will be on the top.

Serves 6

Rum Balls

1½ cup	*cake crumbs or crushed biscuits*
½ cup	*raisins*
1¼ cup	*grated coconut*
¼ cup	*lemon juice (use equal portions of lime and orange juice)*
2 tbsp.	*cocoa powder*
3 tbsp.	*rum*
1 tin	*condensed milk*
	grated coconut, white or discoloured for decoration

1 Mix crushed biscuits or crumbs with raisins, coconut, lemon juice, cocoa and rum.

2 Add enough condensed milk to hold dry ingredients together.

3 Chill and roll into balls.

4 Roll in grated coconut.

5 Store in refrigerator.

Serves 12

Bombay Bouquet

3	*Bombay mangoes*
1 qt.	*vanilla ice cream*
	crushed nuts
	whipped cream

1 Cut chilled Bombay mangoes in halves.

2 Take out seed.

3 Fill cavity with vanilla ice cream or a flavour of your choice.

4 Top with whipped cream and sprinkle with crushed nuts.

Serves 6

Grapefruit Delight

Jamaica's sunny climate seems to develop the sucrose in the citrus, giving rise to the Jamaican phrase 'so sweet it scratch yu throat', which describes sweet citrus. A dessert which belies the ease of preparation and the exotic taste is Grapefruit Delight, grapefruit segments and condensed milk, so simple you could miss trying it. Jamaicans have developed a taste for sweetened condensed milk and use it instead of sugar wherever milk and sugar can be used.

3	*grapefruits*
2 oz.	*condensed milk*
	pinch of nutmeg (optional)

1 Wash grapefruits and cut across in halves.

2 Take out segments carefully leaving skin intact.

3 Mix segments with enough condensed milk to sweeten.

4 Chill segments and shells separately.

5 To serve pour chilled segments back in shells.

6 Sprinkle with nutmeg.

Serves 6

Matrimony

Matrimony is not only a marriage for which you can get a licence after only 24 hours in Jamaica, but also a delicious dessert combining star apples, oranges and condensed milk. Perhaps after tasting it you will discover other reasons why it is called matrimony.

4-6 ripe star apples
4 ripe oranges
1½ cup condensed milk (tins are 14 oz.)
grated nutmeg

1. Cut star apples in halves. Remove seeds and scoop pulp from inside being careful to remove only soft pulp.
2. Place pulp in a bowl.
3. Peel and remove sections from oranges and mix with star apple pulp.
4. Sweeten with condensed milk and chill.
5. To serve, top with grated nutmeg.

Serves 6

Guava Cheese

1½ lb. guava
1 lb. sugar

1. Choose large ripe fruit and pare as thinly as possible.
2. Cut into halves and scoop out seeds.
3. Pound the rind to a fine pulp and rub through a strainer.
4. Add sugar and mix thoroughly. Boil, stirring constantly until the mixture leaves the side of the pan.
5. Pour quickly into shallow dishes. When cold, cut in shapes.
6. Sprinkle with castor sugar and dry in the sun.

Yields 4 cups

Tamarind Balls

These are good as sweets and in sweet and sour dishes.

1 lb. granulated sugar
1 lb. tamarinds

1. Shell tamarinds and rub flesh through a sieve.
2. Mix tamarind flesh with sugar. Knead on a board until mixture becomes light in colour.
3. Roll into small balls.
4. Roll each ball in granulated sugar.
5. Store in airtight glass jars.

Yields 20-24 balls

Toasted Coconut Shell

A quick and easy pastry shell.

2 cups grated coconut
¼ cup butter or margarine

1. Heat oven to 375° F.
2. Place coconut and butter mixture in a 9 inch pie plate.
3. Bake 15 to 20 minutes, stirring very frequently to brown coconut evenly.
4. With the back of a spoon, press over bottom and sides of pie plate.
5. Chill before adding filling.

Baked Bananas with Creme (front)
Matrimony (right)
Quick Orange Ice Cream(left)
Bombay Bouquet (back, right)
Coconut Creme (back, left)

After Dinner Mints

These are known as the popular 'candy bumps' which perhaps gave birth to the saying 'story come to bump' or ready to be told. You will have no problem whatsoever making these if you have a candy thermometer.

2 cups	*sugar*
¾ cup	*water*
4 tbsp.	*butter or margarine*
2 tbsp.	*vinegar*
5-10	*drops oil of peppermint*
	food colouring (optional)

1 Mix all ingredients together.

2 Stir until sugar dissolves.

3 Boil rapidly keeping sides of pan free from crystals.

4 Cook without stirring to hard ball stage (260° F.)

5 Pour on to oiled platter.

6 When cool enough to handle, add colouring as desired.

7 When candy is stiff, stretch on a table, twist into a rope and cut it in 1 inch lengths.

8 Wrap in greased paper and place in an air tight container.

Yields 24

Marshmallows

This recipe for these easy to make marshmallows is for all the teenagers who are addicted to toasted marshmallows, especially my granddaughter, Melissa and her friends. Hope they will experience the thrill of making and enjoying them for many years.

2 cups	*sugar*
¾ cup	*boiling water*
2	*envelopes unflavoured gelatine (2 tablespoons)*
½ cup	*cold water*
½ tsp.	*salt*
1 tsp.	*vanilla*
	icing sugar

1 Add sugar to boiling water until syrup gets to thread stage. Remove from fire. Soften gelatine in cold water.

2 Add gelatine mixture to hot syrup and stir until dissolved. Let stand until partially cooled.

3 Add salt and vanilla.

4 Beat until mixture becomes thick, fluffy and cold.

5 Pour into pans (size about 8 x 4). Make mixture 1 inch in depth.

6 When set cut into desired sizes.

7 Cover thickly with icing sugar.

Yields 24 big marshmallows

CHEERS!

'Take her to Jamaica where the rum come from'.

Rum was born here, and Jamaica produces a greater variety of types and flavours than anywhere else in the world. A Jamaican woman was once asked about the funny sounding name she gave her baby boy, and her reply was that she saw it on a bottle. Yes! You guessed it, it was a rum bottle, and the label could have been her favourite reading matter.

Rum is really the spirit of Jamaica. If Jamaicans are unable to sleep they use it as a night-cap, using the convenient bottle cap to measure even 1 cap in water or their favourite chaser. Headache, stomachache, cuts and bruises of the skin and the heart - white overproof rum is the answer.

Jamaicans love for rum flavours, run the gamut from golden dark sweet, to pale light dry and dates back over three centuries to the early days of British colonization. Before that a more primitive brew was used by the Spanish Conquistadors.

This liquor of the West Indies has certainly seen changes from the seaman's ration and the pirate's grog, to the smooth base now known worldwide and, like wine, is used in drinks and for cooking e.g. in fruit cocktails, sours, stews, sauces, meats, Alexanders, ice creams, as well as puddings, souffles, coffee and delicious wedding cake. In fact, it is not easy to find anything that is not improved by the addition of Jamaican rum, proving its long held reputation as the finest in the world.

Remember it need not be mixed; have it straight, a shot of whites or a QQ (quarter quart) of rum in water.

Planters Punch

In Jamaica, if you farm on a few acres of land, you are called a cultivator, but when you are a large farmer and specialize in one crop, you are called a planter. The lifestyle of one, is very different from that of the other. Long ago, when a cultivator wanted to plant a crop, he had a 'morning sport'. This was a morning when all the neighbours came over to him and concentrated on his field. They would start very early in the morning and as the saying goes 'many hands make light work'. There would be plenty to eat and drink and along with the work, lots of camaraderie, enjoyment and satisfaction. When a planter wanted to plant his crop, 'squire', as he was usually called, employed men to do it, and while they were working, he retired to his easy chair on the shady side of the verandah and had a planters punch and a smoke, before returning to see how the hired hands were progressing.

Here are two recipes for Planters Punch.

Recipe #1:

For each serving use:

1 tbsp.	*lime juice*
1 tbsp.	*syrup*
2 oz.	*dark rum*
1 cup	*soda water or cold water*
	chunks of orange, pineapple and lime
1	*sprig of black mint*

1 In a jug, mix lime juice, syrup and rum.

2 Pour in a tall glass with finely crushed ice.

3 Fill with soda water or cold water and add fruit.

4 Garnish with lime or fresh mint for a long refreshing drink.

Recipe #2:

1 cup	*syrup*
4	*shakes Angostura bitters*
1 qt.	*of dark rum*
1	*large can pineapple juice*

1 In a jug mix syrup, bitters, rum and pineapple juice.

2 Pour in a tall glass with finely crushed ice.

3 Add chopped pineapple and decorate with fresh mint.

Serves 1

Hot Egg Punch

Many churches have Midnight Mass or an early morning service at 5 a.m. on Christmas morning. Egg nog is the traditional drink on Christmas morning and is usually made in quantity. Although there is no snow on the ground at Christmas, the mornings can be nippy so it is usually served hot.

6	*eggs*
	pinch of salt
5 tbsp.	*granulated sugar*
4 cups	*milk*
1 cup	*Jamaica rum or 1 cup brandy*
	grated nutmeg

1 Beat egg yolks with mixer until thick and lemon coloured. Add salt and sugar.

2 Gradually pour a small amount of heated milk into egg mixture, so it will not cook the eggs. Continue to add milk until the eggs are almost the same temperature as the milk, then pour in all at once.

3 Add rum and brandy as required.

4 Sprinkle with grated nutmeg and serve.

Serves 6

Cook's Tip

If doing a small quantity of the mixture, pour in the blender and mix. Unless you are serving all at once, do not mix all ingredients. Some people may not want the amount of spirit, so omit and pour in as required. White rum is usually used for this purpose, but many prefer the less harsh red rum in egg nog.

Chilled Egg Nog

Use same ingredients as hot punch; you may reduce milk to 3 cups and add 1 cup cream.

1 Separate eggs and beat the yolk until thick.

2 Gradually beat in sugar and rum or brandy. A shaving of lime rind may be best.

3 Allow to rest.

4 When ready to serve, blend in milk, stiffly beaten egg whites and cream, and add grated nutmeg.

Serve 6

Sorrel

White sorrel is becoming very popular, but most households still use red sorrel at Christmas. There are many recipes for drawing sorrel and nearly all use root ginger and cinnamon leaves or spice.

Here are two recipes. Perhaps you would like to try them both.

Recipe #1:

3 lb.	*sorrel*
1 in.	*root ginger, washed, crushed and blended*
12	*whole cloves*
5	*pimento leaves, or 4 green dried grains of pimento*
6	*cinnamon leaves*
6 pt.	*boiling water*
½ cup	*overproof rum (optional)*
½ lb.	*granulated sugar or sweeten to taste*
1 tbsp.	*lime juice*
1 tbsp.	*rice*

1 Cut sorrel sepals from seeds and wash well.

2 Put sepals in a crock jar with ginger, cloves, pimento and cinnamon leaves.

3 Pour on boiling water, cover with a cloth and set aside for 24 hours.

4 A tablespoon of rice can be put in sorrel to speed fermentation.

5 Strain and sweeten with granulated sugar and a little lime juice. You may add the rum at this point.

6 Bottle and chill.

Recipe #2:

3 cups	*picked sorrel (sorrel is now sold picked and ready for drawing)*
1 in.	*root ginger*
12	*whole cloves*
3	*pimento leaves*
4	*cinnamon leaves*
5 cups	*boiling water*
½ lb.	*brown sugar or sweeten to taste*

1 Add sorrel, ginger, cloves and spice leaves to rapidly boiling water. Keep on fire and allow water to return to a boil.

2 Simmer for a further 4 minutes.

3 Strain and sweeten.

4 Bottle.

Yields 12 cups

Cook's Tip

Frozen sorrel gives better results than dried sorrel: better flavour, better colour.

Fruit Punch

6 cups	*orange juice*
2 cups	*pineapple juice*
1 cup	*guava nectar*
1 cup	*tea*
	strawberry syrup (optional)

1 Mix together all ingredients and bottle. Leave at least 30 minutes. Serve over ice.

Serves 10

Ice Breaker

1	*bottle red wine*
2	*whole cloves*
1 in.	*cinnamon stick*
3 in.	*lime peel*
¾ cup	*sugar*
1 cup	*water*
6-8 oz.	*rum*

1 Place all ingredients except rum in a saucepan and bring to boil.

2 Place 1 oz. rum in each heatproof glass, if glass is not heatproof, put a spoon in it, and pour hot wine mixture on the spoon in the glass. Serve over ice.

Serves 6-8

Carrot Drink

2 cups	*diced carrots*
2 cups	*water*
1 cup	*evaporated milk*
7 tbsp.	*granulated sugar*
¼ tsp.	*nutmeg*
1 tsp.	*vanilla*
4 cubes	*ice*

1 Add carrots to water in blender.

2 Cover and blend for 30 seconds, until carrot is blended.

3 Strain and rinse blender jar.

4 Pour strained juice back in blender and add remaining ingredients.

5 Blend again and serve chilled.

Serves 6

Cook's Tip
Carrots can be cooked before blending, but the taste is slightly different to the drink made with raw carrots.

Beetroot Drink

1 cup	*diced beetroot*
2 cups	*water*
¼ tsp.	*nutmeg*
2 tbsp.	*condensed milk*

1 Place water and diced beetroots in blender.

2 Cover and blend fine. Strain.

3 Rinse blender. Pour in strained juice, other ingredients and three cubes of ice.

4 Blend for 10 more seconds and serve cold.

Serves 4-6

Garden Cherry Drink

2 cups garden cherries
1 cup water
1 cup sugar

1 Wash cherries. Combine water and cherries and allow to stand for 30 minutes.

2 Strain mixture through coarse sieve. Sweeten and put all ingredients in blender. Blend on low speed.

3 Strain and chill.

Serves 2

Otaheite Apple Drink

12 ripe apples
1 lb. granulated sugar
1 qt. water
½ oz. root ginger
juice of 2 limes

1 Wash fruit and ginger.

2 Grate ginger and set aside.

3 Add sugar to water.

4 Chop apples and sprinkle with lime juice.

5 Add apples and ginger to water. Bring to the boil and simmer for about 20 minutes.

6 Cool, strain and sweeten..

7 Serve with crushed ice.

Serves 8

Soursop Juice

1 one ripe soursop
condensed milk
nutmeg
½ tsp. lime juice
3 cups water

1 Remove skin from soursop.

2 Place 3 cups of water and 1 cup of soursop pulp (seeds included) in blender.

3 Blend for 2 seconds on the lowest speed, turning blender on and off, in order not to crush seeds, but to take off pulp.

4 Strain and remove seeds.

5 You may return pulp to the juice to make a thicker drink but it does not enhance the flavour very much more.

6 Sweeten with condensed milk, a dash of nutmeg and about ½ teaspoon lime juice.

7 Serve with cracked ice.

Serves 3-4

Cook's Tip

This is the way most Jamaicans make soursop drink but a more refreshing drink can be made by sweetening the juice with sugar and limes and serving over cracked ice.

Lemonade

'Wash' as in lemonade, could mean a mixture of brown sugar and water. In this land of sugarcane and sun, 'wash' is a welcome drink. Add limes to wash and you get lemonade.

The way we combine water, lime, sugar and ice makes quite a difference to lemonade.

3 tbsp.	*sugar*
1 pt.	*water*
2	*limes*

1 Mix water and sugar.

2 Add lime juice before adding lots of crushed ice.

3 Serve with flair in sparkling, attractive glasses.

Serves 10-12

Cook's Tip

If you add the lime juice or ice to the water before adding sugar, you will use more sugar to sweeten the lemonade than if you mix the water and the sugar first.

Sparkling Tea Punch

2 cups	*cold strong tea*
3 tbsp.	*sugar*
2 tbsp.	*lime juice*
2 cups	*ginger beer*

1 Stir tea and sugar until mixed, then add lime juice.

2 Just before serving, add ginger beer.

3 Serve with ice, garnished with a slice of lime.

Serves 4

Rum Punch

Jamaican rum conjures up warm sensations, as warm as this sunny isle. The blend of our limes, with the special flavoured syrups we manufacture, combine to make a punch second to none. If you are a visitor and would like to stretch your precious bottle of rum, this is the most delicious way.

The rhyme says 'one of sour, two of sweet, three of strong and four of weak'.

1 One of sour is 1 measure of lime juice.

2 Two of sweet is 1 measure of granulated sugar and 1 measure of syrup.

3 Three of strong is 3 measures of rum.

4 Four of weak is 4 measures of water. Measures can be tablespoons or gallon bottles but always use the same ratio of one to the other.

5 Mix all ingredients thoroughly together and serve over ice.

Cook's Tip

To this basic recipe, you may add a pinch of salt, some grated nutmeg, or 6 pimento berries. Fruit juice may be added as a portion of water. Bottle and cork well. The mixture improves with age, so mix it early before ready to use and allow it to mature. One warning - be careful - a taste of this heady brew is very addictive!

Ginger Beer

Recipe #1:

2 oz.	*root ginger, grated or blended*
2½ lb.	*granulated sugar*
1 oz.	*cream of tartar*
	juice of 8 limes
10 qt.	*boiling water*

1 Mix all ingredients together. Cover and leave for a day or two.

Yields 24 servings

Recipe #2:

1 oz.	*green ginger*
4 qt.	*water*
1½ lb.	*sugar*
½	*lemon*
¼ oz.	*cream of tartar*
1 oz.	*dry yeast*

1 Pound the ginger and put in water.

2 Add the sugar and boil for about 1 hour.

3 Skim and add the sliced lemon and cream of tartar.

4 When almost cold, stir in yeast.

5 After 2 days, strain and bottle. Use in a day or two.

Serves 10-12

Orange Syrup

The following syrups are excellent for use in mixed drinks.

1 cup	*orange juice*
2 cups	*sugar*
2 tbsp.	*grated orange rind*

1 Combine juice, sugar and rind in a saucepan.

2 Stir over low heat until sugar is dissolved.

3 Cook for 5 minutes.

Yields 12 oz.

Lime Syrup

½ cup	*lime juice*
1 cup	*sugar*
1 tbsp.	*grated lime rind*

1 Combine lime juice, sugar and rind in a saucepan.

2 Stir over low heat until sugar is dissolved.

3 Cook for 5 minutes.

Yields 8 oz.

Sugar Syrup

2 cups	*sugar*
2 cups	*water*

1 Cook over low heat until thick.

2 Bottle and use for lemonade and other mixed drinks.

Yields 12-14 oz.

Lime Squash

Lenice Madan of the Liguanea Club in Kingston thinks this is a perfect drink for lunch.

1 oz.	*lime juice*
2 oz.	*sugar syrup*
4 oz.	*soda water*

1 Put all ingredients with ice in a 12 oz. Collins glass.

2 Stir with bar spoon.

3 Serve with a long straw and a cherry.

Serves 1

Limeade

1 oz.	*lime juice*
2 oz.	*sugar syrup*
4 oz.	*water*

1 Mix as for lime squash.

Serves 1

Piña Colada with Coconut Rum

1/4 oz.	*sugar syrup*
2 oz.	*evaporated cream*
3 oz.	*pineapple juice*
	dash cinnamon and nutmeg
3 drops	*Angostura bitters*
1/4 oz.	*Apricot brandy*
1 oz.	*coconut rum*

1 Blend all ingredients in crushed ice.

2 Serve in 12 oz. Collins glass with 1 pineapple slice, 1 cherry and a long straw.

Serves 1

Rum Sour

3/4 oz.	*lime juice*
1/4 oz.	*sugar syrup*
1 oz.	*rum*

1 Shake or blend ingredients with crushed ice.

2 Serve in 7 oz. rock glass with 1 slice lime.

Serves 1

Big Bamboo

1/2 oz.	*lime juice*
1/4 oz.	*sugar syrup*
1 oz.	*dark rum*
1 oz.	*light rum*
1/4 oz.	*Tia Maria*
3 oz.	*pineapple juice*

1 Shake or blend ingredients with crushed ice.

2 Serve in 12 oz. Collins glass with 1 pineapple slice, 1 orange slice, 1 cherry and a long straw.

Serves 1

Yellow Bird

1/2 oz.	*lime juice*
1/4 oz.	*sugar syrup*
3 oz.	*orange juice*
1/4 oz.	*Tia Maria*
1 oz.	*rum*
1/4 oz.	*creme de banane*
3 oz.	*galliano liqueur*

1 Shake or blend ingredients together with ice cubes.

2 Pour into 12 oz. Collins glass with 1 pineapple slice, 1 orange slice, 1 cherry and a long straw.

Serves 1

Shandy

1	*bottle dry ginger ale, ginger beer or lemonade*
1	*bottle cold beer*

1 Combine beer with equal quantities of lemonade, ginger beer or dry ginger ale.

2 Serve over ice

Serves 2

Mint Julep

	sprig of mint for each glass
2 tsp.	*granulated sugar*
	whisky

1 Bruise mint and put in glass.

2 Add sugar.

3 Half fill glass with ice.

4 Add whisky to taste.

5 Stand in refrigerator for an hour or more.

Serves 1

Brown Cow

2 oz.	*evaporated milk*
1 oz.	*brown coffee liqueur or creme de cacao*

1 Mix ingredients together and serve with crushed ice.

2 Pour into 9 oz. rock glass.

3 Serve with a straw.

Serves 1

Pink Lady

2 oz.	*evaporated milk*
1 oz.	*strawberry fruit syrup*
1 oz.	*gin*

1 Mix all ingredients with cubed ice and blend.

2 Strain into 5½ oz. champagne glass.

3 Serve with a short straw.

Serves 1

Banana Daiquiri

1 tbsp.	*lime juice*
1 tsp.	*plain or sugar syrup*
2 tbsp.	*rum*
1	*small ripe banana*

1 Blend all ingredients together until smooth.

2 Serve over crushed ice.

Serves 1

Orange Liqueur

12	*oranges (include 2 Seville or sour oranges)*
3 lb.	*granulated sugar*
2 ½	*cups rum*

1 Wash, dry and peel oranges thinly.

2 Squeeze and strain juice.

3 Put the peel and sugar in alternate layers in an earthenware or glass jar.

4 Add rum.

5 Cover the jar tightly and leave in a warm place for about three weeks, shaking the mixture occasionally.

6 Strain off the liquid.

7 Bottle and cork well.

Serves 18-20

Cook's Tip

This liqueur improves with age.

Ginger Wine

¼ lb.	*ginger*
4 lb.	*dark sugar*
4 qt.	*water, boiled and cooled to 110° F.*
2 tsp.	*yeast*
½ lb.	*dried fruit*
½ oz.	*mace*

1 Crush ginger and put into jar.

2 Add all other ingredients and leave for 21 days.

3 Strain and bottle.

Yields approximately 4 bottles

Pimento Liqueur

I am very grateful to Killie and Helen Urquhart for supplying me with ripe pimento berries over the years for making this liqueur.

1 pt.	*ripe pimento berries*
3 lb.	*granulated sugar*
1 pt.	*white rum*
1½ pt.	*boiling water*
¼ oz.	*cinnamon stick*
¼ cup	*lemon/lime juice*

1 Lightly bruise and soak ripe pimento berries in rum for 14 days.

2 Dissolve sugar in water and cool.

3 Boil cinnamon stick in a little water (about ½ cup to extract flavour.)

4 Strain.

5 Add to syrup, then add lime juice.

6 Pour rum off the berries.

7 Mix all together, strain and bottle.

Serves 18-20

Cook's Tip

If too sweet add more rum. Drop a few raisins in each bottle.

Rice Wine

½ lb.	*paddy rice (unshelled rice)*
	Peel or zest from one orange
¾ lb.	*raisins*
¼ lb.	*prunes*
2 lb.	*clear (dark) sugar*
¼	*yeast cake or quarter pack of dried yeast*
½	*of an orange, sliced and peeled*
2 qts.	*water, boiled and cooled*

1 Wash rice.

2 Add peel from one orange.

3 Place in jar along with other ingredients.

4 Set aside for 1 year.

5 Strain and bottle.

Yields 3 bottles

> **Cook's Tip**
> Before bottling, rinse bottles with proof rum. Shelled rice may be used if paddy rice is unavailable.

Tangerine Liqueur

12	*large orange skins*
	or
18	*small orange skins*
2 qt.	*gin*
3 lb.	*granulated sugar*
1 qt.	*cold water*

1 Wash skins and soak in 2 qt. gin for 24-48 hours.

2 Strain and set aside.

3 Boil granulated sugar and 1 qt. cold water for 10 minutes.

4 Mix syrup with gin mixture.

5 Cool bottle and label.

6 Leave for about 30 days before drinking.

Yields 2 bottles

Tangerine Wine

2 qt.	*tangerine or ortanique juice*
2 lb.	*brown sugar*
1 pt.	*lime juice*
1 qt.	*white Jamaican rum*
1 cup	*milk*
2 tbsp.	*crushed egg shells*

1 Mix first 4 ingredients together and put in clean glass bottle for 3 days.

2 Add milk, egg shells.

3 Stir and leave for 4 days.

4 Strain, bottle and label.

Yields 4 bottles

Essentials for The Real Taste of JAMAICA

Coconut Milk

Coconut milk is an essential ingredient for many traditional Jamaican recipes. It may be purchased in a can but it is quite easy to make your own and considerably cheaper.

1	*dry coconut*
	water (some people use cold, some use hot)

1 Extract water from coconut by punching a hole in one of the eyes. (This helps to make the dry shell crack and the flesh is much easier to remove.)

2 Ease the flesh from the shell.

3 Grate coconut flesh or cut up and blend in blender or food processor with water, until pureed.

4 Squeeze mixture through strainer to extract milk. The flavour and strength of the milk depends on the amount of water used to squeeze the milk from the grated coconut.

Yields about ½ cup

Pita Bread Toast

Served with many kinds of soups.

2	*pita breads*
2 oz.	*soft butter*

1 Use scissors to cut each bread in 12 wedges.

2 Separate and butter each wedge lightly on the rough side.

3 Put on an ungreased cookie sheet and crisp in a warm oven, about 300° F. They get crisp and burn in a very short time if the oven is any hotter. Bread should not be brown.

4 Serve hot or cold. They can be done ahead of serving time and stored in an airtight jar.

Yields 12

Johnny Cakes

Some people call these fried dumplings whilst others say fried Johnny cakes. Whatever they are uncertain about, it is not the eating of it. This recipe I collected in Antigua, at Sir Lascelles and Lady Robotham's. The recipe used in Jamaica, is kneaded much more and as a result is much harder.

2 cups	*flour*
2 tbsp.	*sugar*
¼ tsp.	*salt*
1 tbsp.	*baking powder*
2 tbsp.	*margarine or butter*
½ cup	*cooking oil*
½ cup	*milk or water*

1 Mix all ingredients, except milk, until the butter blends in with the flour evenly.

2 Add a little milk at a time until a firm dough is formed.

3 Divide dough into balls (about a tbsp. in size each). Knead each one from the outside in for ½ a minute.

4 Press gently with hands and fry in oil. Drain and serve hot.

Serves 6

Spinners

Jamaicans love these in many kinds of soups, and stew peas and rice would not be the same without them.

1 cup	*flour*
	pinch of salt
	enough water to make a stiff dough

1 Mix ingredients together to make a stiff dough.

2 Pinch off ½ oz. of dough.

3 Knead and shape in palm of hands into a long, fairly thin dumpling. Repeat. Allow to stew in soup about 15 minutes before serving.

Festival

An essential accompaniment to jerk pork and fried fish, Festival is the Jamaican equivalent of a Hush Puppy.

1 cup	*yellow cornmeal*
1 cup	*all-purpose flour*
2 tsp.	*baking powder*
1 tbsp.	*sugar*
½ tsp.	*salt*
1	*egg, beaten*
	ice water
	oil for frying

1 Mix ingredients together and add enough ice water to make a soft dough but firm enough to be able to shape in long dumplings. Knead lightly. Divide dough into 6 portions and roll each portion into 6 x 2 inch lengths. Make middle of festival flat so it will cook evenly.

2 Fry in deep fat or hot oil 1 inch deep until golden brown, turning when necessary.

3 Drain on paper towel.

4 Serve hot.

Serves 6

Helpful Hints

Poultry

To season and prepare chicken for cooking:

1 Clean inside of chicken well. Wash in vinegar or lime water and drain. Draining is very important as water dilutes the seasoning.

2 Allow a tsp. of salt for each lb. of poultry. For a 3 lb. chicken mix 3 tsp. salt, 1 tsp. sugar, ½ tsp. black pepper and set aside.

3 Before putting on dry seasoning, mix 2 cloves garlic with 2 stalks escallion, finely chopped and a sprig of thyme with a little vinegar or water. (Can be blended with blender.)

4 Spread garlic mixture on chicken and allow to stay for 10 minutes before putting on dry seasoning. Allow to marinate for at least ½ hour.

To debone chicken:

A friend of mine after deboning a chicken for a dinner party kept the carcass in her freezer as proof of the feat for about six months, so pleased was she with her achievement.

1 Clean chicken well. Wash in vinegar or lime water and wipe dry.

2 Position the chicken with back upward and cut through skin on the backbone from neck to tail with sharp pointed knife.

3 Cut off the wing tips and cut skin from around the cut off portion of the wing tips.

4 Cut skin around the legs to allow the meat to slip off the bones.

5 Working from the cut in the back, remove flesh as far as centre front, working from right to left. Remove the wing and thigh bones from the inside, scraping downwards - **do not cut through the skin over the breast bone.**

6 Turn the chicken around and work on the other half.

7 Push the skin of the legs and wings inside. Cut away the 'Parson's nose', as we call the oil sack, and any sinews from the legs.

8 Wash, drain and season the inside well. The bones from the carcass and wing tips can make a chicken stock or gravy.

Fish

Fish cooks in a very short time and as soon as the flesh turns opaque, it is ready to be served. It is very easy to overcook fish.

A fillet is a piece of fish without skin and bones. Fillets look better on the serving plates if they are approximately the same size. Rolled fillets are called turbans. Wooden toothpicks are used to keep fillets in shape during cooking, but the picks are removed before serving. Remember to soak wooden toothpicks in water before using.

How to prepare fish for cooking:

1 First clean and scale the fish. Always use newspaper to protect table and board. Hold the fish by the tail and with the blade of a knife or a potato peeler, scrape off the scales, working towards the head.

2 Make an incision through the belly of the fish. Grasp the end of the intestine nearest the head and pull it away along the length of the slit. Cut the intestine at the tail end.

3 Kitchen scissors do a very good job of cutting off fins and trimming tails. Using the scissors, cut off the back fin and the side, lower and tail fins. If head is to be left on, remove the eyes (if you wish).

4 Jamaican cooks generally wash the fish in lime and water, making sure that the cavity is thoroughly cleaned. Most people who live by the sea claim sea water is better to prepare fish for cooking. Lift on to a cloth and dry.

5 Season with garlic, salt and black pepper allowing ½ a tsp. of salt for each lb. of fish. Other seasonings usually go in the sauce served with the fish.

To debone fish:

1 Gut and trim the fish

2 Insert a sharp knife close to the backbone at the tail end and cut the flesh from the bone, working towards the head and keeping the knife as close as possible to the bone. Small bones that adhere to the flesh or are embedded in it, must be removed with tweezers or the fingers.

To fillet fish:

1 Gut and trim the fish.

2 Place the fish on a wet kitchen towel to prevent slippage. Keep fish steady with one hand. Trim fins with scissors or sharp knife.

3 Insert the point of the knife in the back, close to the head, cut down the back on top of the backbone. Lift off the top fillet.

4 Now slip the knife under the bone at the head and keeping it as close as possible to the backbone, work down to the tail using short, sharp strokes, at the same time keeping a firm hold on the head with the other hand. Lift out backbone.

Shellfish

How to prepare lobster for cooking:

1 When confronted by a live lobster, look for a pot with a lid large enough to hold it. (Even better if you have a steamer.) Put water to boil and when it is on a rollicking boil, put in lobster. Have lid standing by to cover as soon as it goes in the water - this is for your protection from the steaming water. As soon as it comes back to a boil, time it and cook for only 7 minutes more.

2 Rinse boiled lobster.

(For grilled lobster split tails lengthwise along back.)

3 Twist off head from tail. Remove liver, roe and stomach.

4 Twist off claws where they join the body. Using a nutcracker or hammer, remove the flesh from the claws.

5 Release flesh from tails keeping end still attached. Remove intestinal vein beneath flesh of centre back, rinse and return to shell. (For Lobster Newburgh, detach flesh completely from tail, wash shell and keep, rinse and cut up meat into large cubes.)

How to prepare shrimp for cooking:

1 Twist off head and remove shell.

2 Remove vein (intestine) out of centre back.

3 Rinse.

Garnishing Ideas

Here is a guide to which vegetables to use with which meats.

Beef

Cabbage, cauliflower, green beans, tomatoes, beets, mushrooms, eggplant, turnip.

Pork

Cabbage, cauliflower, celery, callaloo and other greens, tomatoes, sweet potatoes.

Ham

Same as pork, also string beans.

Fish

Tomatoes, peas, string beans, cucumber.

Lamb

Carrots, peas, chocho, cauliflower, turnips.

Veal

Beets, eggplant, chocho, mushrooms.

Chicken

Corn, peas, sweet potatoes, lima beans.

Turkey

Creamed onions, sweet potatoes, sprouts.

Garnishing ideas for Fish and Meats

Fish

Lemon wedges or lemon slices sprinkled with parsley

Minced sweet pepper or scotch bonnet pepper

Orange slices

Grapefruit sections

Thick slices of small cucumber

Tomato slices topped with thin slices of lemon or limes

Stuffed olives.

Meats

Pork

Apple sauce; stuffed black prunes; slices of orange with cress or parsley.

Chicken

Bunches of grapes; moulded cranberry cut out on orange slices (also with turkey).

Lamb

Green mint jelly in canned pear halves.

Ham

Pineapples; orange slices; spiced pear halves and water cress.

Steak

Sauteed mushroom caps; French fried onion rings.

Beef

Glazed onions; buttered carrot strips; prepared mustard in tomato caps.

Secrets For Successful Baking

1 When making cakes select good ingredients.

2 If you are using a recipe in liquid cups, check if recipe is English or American. 1 English cup is 10 oz. whereas 1 American cup is 8 oz.

3 A dry measuring cup is filled to the top for measuring 1 cup whereas a liquid measuring cup is filled to the 1 cup mark and allowance left to prevent spilling.

4 Check if recipe calls for single or double acting baking powder.

5 Collect all ingredients and baking pans before starting. Have shortening at room temperature, if room is not too hot. Cream shortening but do not melt, if recipe calls for creaming.

6 Add sugar slowly (about a tbsp. at a time).

7 If adding egg yolks, they can be added beaten or unbeaten and not all at once.

8 Add flavouring in the creaming mixture. It will mix in evenly and avoid being omitted from mixture.

9 Sift flour before measuring, then sift again with baking powder, salt and spices if used together. Add alternately with milk or other liquid. Add ½ cup of dry ingredients to mixture first, then some of the milk or other liquid. Add flour in 4 and milk in 3, beginning and ending with flour. Water is a good substitute for milk, but milk is better than fruit juices.

10 Fold in beaten egg white - until entirely blended with the batter. Do this carefully with a rubber scraper. Do not over mix to break air bubbles.

11 Bake in greased pans in moderate oven (remember to grease all layer, cups, loaf and cake pans with unsalted oil or butter.) Fill pans ⅔ full of batter, place in oven previously heated about 10 mins. to required temperature. If sides of layer tins are not greased the cake will rise more evenly. Do not open oven door before end of baking time, if oven heat is reliable.

12 When cake is done, it shrinks from the sides of pan, springs back when pressed lightly on top with finger or does not stick to cake tester, toothpick or knife when inserted in centre.

13 Dark tins turn out darker cakes than light tins. Stainless steel tins are easier to clean and stay shinier longer but you may find aluminium tins give good results.

14 Chocolate contains more fat than cocoa, so where cocoa is substituted in a cake, use 3½ tablespoons cocoa and add ½ tablespoon butter for each ounce or square of chocolate. Either sift cocoa with dry ingredients, or mix with just enough milk or water to make a paste and add directly after eggs or egg yolks.

Capacities of Bottles

A bottle of table wine gives about 6 glasses

A bottle of champagne gives about 8 glasses

A bottle of sherry or port gives about 12 glasses

A bottle of whisky, gin, brandy or rum gives about 26 glasses

A bottle of liqueur gives about 32 glasses

Easy Imperial-Metric Conversion Chart

All quantities used in the recipes in this book are in imperial measures. For convenience the conversion from imperial to metric measures has been rounded off into units of 25 grams. See table below for recommended equivalents. All recipes use an American measuring cup; the British measuring cup is slightly larger. Never mix metric and imperial measures in one recipe. Always use level measures.

Dry Measures

Imperial	Recommended Metric conversion
1 oz.	25 g.
2 oz.	50 g.
3 oz.	75 g.
4 oz.	100 g.
8 oz.	225 g.
12 oz.	350 g.
16 oz. (1 lb.)	450 g.
20 oz. (1 1/4 lb.)	575 g.
2 lb 3 oz.	1000 g. (1 kg.)

Liquid or Volume Measures

Imperial	Recommended Metric conversion
1/2 tsp.	2 ml..
1 tsp.	5 ml.
1 tbsp.	15 ml.
1 fl oz. (2 tbsp.)	30 ml.
2 fl oz.	50 ml.
5 fl oz. (1/4 pt.)	150 ml.
1/2 pt.	300 ml.
1 pt.	600 ml.
1 3/4 pt.	1000 ml. (1 litre)

Imperial Measure	American cups
1 lb. butter or margarine	2 cups
1 lb. flour	4 cups
1 lb. granulated or castor sugar	2 cups
1 lb. brown sugar	2 cups
1 lb. icing sugar	3 cups
1 lb. rice	2-2 1/2 cups

Oven Temperatures

°F	°C
200-250	110-130
250-300	130-150
300-350	150-180
350-370	180-190
375-400	190-200
425-450	220-230
450-500	230-240

INDEX